RODALE ORGANIC GARDENING
SOLUTIONS

RODALE ORGANIC GARDENING
SOLUTIONS

Over 500 Answers to Real-Life Questions from Backyard Gardeners

CHERYL LONG and the editors of **ORGANIC GARDENING** magazine

RODALE

RODALE
WE INSPIRE AND ENABLE PEOPLE TO IMPROVE
THEIR LIVES AND THE WORLD AROUND THEM

Library of Congress Cataloging-in-Publication Data

Long, Cheryl.

  Rodale organic gardening solutions : over 500 answers to real life questions from backyard gardeners / Cheryl Long and the editors of Organic gardening magazine.

     p. cm.

  Includes bibliographical references (p.   ) and index.

   ISBN 0–87596–851–1 (hardcover : acid-free paper) — ISBN 0–87596–852–X (pbk. : acid-free paper)

  1. Organic gardening—Miscellanea. I. Rodale (Firm) II. Title.

  SB453.5 .L66 2000   635'.0484—dc21

  00–008144

Distributed in the book trade by St. Martin's Press

2 4 6 8 10 9 7 5 3   hardcover
2 4 6 8 10 9 7 5 3 1 paperback

Editor: Christine Bucks

Back Cover and Interior Book Designer: Marta Mitchell Strait

Front Cover Designer: Christin Gangi

Cover and Interior Illustrator: Michael Klein

Layout Designer: Pat Mast

Computer Graphics Specialist: Dale Mack

Researcher: Diana Erney

Copy Editor: Nancy N. Bailey

Manufacturing Coordinator: Mark Krahforst

Indexer: Lina B. Burton

Editorial Assistance: Kerrie A. Cadden

RODALE ORGANIC GARDENING BOOKS

Managing Editor: Fern Marshall Bradley

Executive Creative Director: Christin Gangi

Art Director: Patricia Field

Production Manager: Robert V. Anderson Jr.

Studio Manager: Leslie M. Keefe

Associate Copy Manager: Jennifer Hornsby

Manufacturing Manager: Mark Krahforst

We're always happy to hear from you. For questions or comments concerning the editorial content of this book, please write to:

Rodale Book Readers' Service
33 East Minor Street
Emmaus, PA 18098

Look for other Rodale books wherever books are sold. Or call us at (800) 848-4735.

For more information about Rodale Organic Gardening magazine and books, visit us at:

www.organicgardening.com

RODALE
Organic Gardening
Starts Here!

Here at Rodale, we've been gardening organically for more than 50 years—ever since my grandfather J. I. Rodale learned about composting and decided that healthy living starts with healthy soil. In 1940 J. I. started the Rodale Organic Farm to test his theories, and today the nonprofit Rodale Institute Experimental Farm is still at the forefront of organic gardening and farming research. In 1942 J. I. founded *Organic Gardening* magazine to share his discoveries with gardeners everywhere. His son, my father, Robert Rodale, headed *Organic Gardening* until 1990, and today a fourth generation of Rodales is growing up with the magazine. Over the years we've shown millions of readers how to grow bountiful crops and beautiful flowers using nature's own techniques.

In this book, you'll find the latest organic methods and the best gardening advice. We know—because all our authors and editors are passionate about gardening! We feel strongly that our gardens should be safe for our children, pets, and the birds and butterflies that add beauty and delight to our lives and landscapes. Our gardens should provide us with fresh, flavorful vegetables, delightful herbs, and gorgeous flowers. And they should be a pleasure to work in as well as to view.

Sharing the secrets of safe, successful gardening is why we publish books. So come visit us at the Rodale Institute Experimental Farm, where you can tour the gardens every day—we're open year-round. And use this book to create your best garden ever.

Happy gardening!

Maria Rodale

Maria Rodale
Rodale Organic Gardening Books

CONTENTS

YOUR PROBLEMS SOLVED!

At *Organic Gardening* magazine, one of the things we like most is learning new tips and tricks about gardening. And with every issue, we uncover something new when we research and write the answers to our readers' questions for the column called "Solutions." Whether it's finding a way to fix a smelly compost pile or what to do about flavorless tomatoes, the information in "Solutions" is often brand-new—even to our experienced gardening staff. That's what keeps gardening exciting!

The gardeners who read *Organic Gardening* magazine feel the same way we do: "Solutions" is one of their favorite parts of the magazine. And that's what led to the birth of this book. We figured every gardener could benefit from the wealth of great gardening information that we've collected in the "Solutions" column.

Here you'll find more than 10 years' worth of "Solutions" columns. All the questions are from backyard gardeners just like yourself, with advice from people in the know—such as university professors, botanists, and horticulturists. The book is divided into nine chapters, including ones on flowers, composting, seed starting and saving, and vegetables. Within each chapter you'll find answers to questions such as whether you should plant beans twice in the same place in your garden, what to do with potted daffodils after they bloom, and what those white spots on your raspberries mean.

Scattered throughout the chapters, you'll find a box called "Check It Out!"—fun "did-you-know" kinds of stuff, such as how adding rosemary to your potatoes will get them to last longer in storage.

We've also included a comprehensive "Resources" listing in the back of the book. That way, if you can't find the seeds, plants, or gardening supplies mentioned in the answers locally, you can order them from some of the mail-order suppliers we've listed. You'll also find source information for specialized products right in some of the answers. And we've included a thorough index for those of you with specific questions, so that you can easily find the page that addresses the problem you need solved.

No matter where you live, or what your level of gardening prowess, *Rodale Organic Gardening Solutions* will give you great advice you can use. From tips on growing vegetables, flowers, and fruit to simplifying lawn care and keeping pests and weeds under control, you'll find comprehensive information on every page. And we hope that advice will help you make the most of the time you spend gardening, so that the rewards— beautiful gardens full of fruit, flowers, and vegetables—will be plentiful.

VEGETABLES

No matter how long you've been gardening, you're bound to have a question or two. For instance, why are your cabbage transplants disappearing? What's the difference between hybrids and open-pollinated veggies? Once you know the answers, you'll be better equipped for turning out a more productive harvest.

VEGETABLES

GENERAL VEGGIE QUESTIONS

Open-Pollinated or Not?

Q: *How can I tell if a vegetable variety is open-pollinated or a hybrid?*

A: Open any seed catalog. If a plant variety is not designated a hybrid (either in the variety name itself or in the catalog description), it's an open-pollinated variety. Such classification is serious business. The sale of seeds is regulated by state and federal labeling laws that protect consumers and help them buy exactly what they want.

Hybrids are sometimes indicated by the term "F1" instead of the word "hybrid." This means the seeds are from the first generation of hybrid plants produced by specific and carefully selected parents. (F2 and succeeding generations are less stable and aren't sold because they won't produce what you want in a variety.) Seed packets and containers must also be marked if the contents are hybrid, says Dave Lambert, executive vice president of the American Seed Trade Association.

About Genetics

Q: *Please explain to me the difference between "genetically engineered" vegetables and vegetables that have been hybridized. Why is one type supposed to be bad and the other acceptable?*

A: In the beginning, there was natural selection. This is what happens when plants are left to their own devices and are pollinated by wind, rain, insects, or birds. Because these chance crossings have been happening for millions of years, the germ plasm of these open-pollinated plants has stabilized. In other words, you can plant their seeds and get plants that are basically the same as the parent plants.

Humans have been involved with plant selection since ancient times, when they gathered some of their food from wild plants. Gradually, people learned to manipulate habitats to increase the size and yield of certain food plants, resulting in the domestication of these plants, or the creation of forms that are different from those found in the wild.

Eventually, people learned how to produce special plants by allowing two selected, closely related parents to cross-pollinate. This is called hybridization. Whenever you want seeds of that special plant (hybrid), you have to isolate the two specific parents so you get genetic material only from those specific sources. That's why you get a lot of surprises when you collect and plant the seeds of a hybrid that has matured in your garden and not in isolation.

Plants make hybrids among themselves all the time, but the science of plant breeding did not begin until Gregor Mendel showed how genetic traits were inherited. (He observed the results of specific pairings of garden peas and published his paper in 1866.)

Genetically engineered plants are a giant step beyond hybrids, which, as we mentioned, are the result of two closely related plants being crossed. Scientists now have the ability to determine exactly which genes control every characteristic of every living organism—and they have developed techniques that allow them to take genes from any animal, plant, bacteria, or virus and transfer the genes into another organism. Genetic engineering is an unnatural technology with unprecedented power to "engineer" the nature of any living organism.

The debate over whether genetic engineering is good or bad is raging among the world's scientists. On one side are those who see genetic engineering as a boon to humankind, with the potential to end hunger, improve health, reduce pesticide use, and conserve natural resources. On the other are those who think the speed at which genetic engineering is showing up in laboratories, fields, and kitchens is unethical and unsafe. They point out that creating a whole new class of plants could have far-ranging, unintended effects.

Expert Advice Wanted

Q: *I'm considering growing herbs, flowers, and specialty crops for market. I need advice and informed opinions.*

A: Your best bet is to talk with organic growers in your area who are already doing what you'd like to do. To get in touch with a few, contact the Organic Crop Improvement Association International (OCIA), a group that certifies organic growers. You can reach them at 1001 Y Street, Suite B, Lincoln, NE 68508-1172; (402) 477-2323; fax: (402) 477-4325; e-mail: info@ocia.org. Your local agricultural extension office may also be able to put you in touch with organic growers in your area.

Don't overlook your state agriculture department and trade groups such as the International Herb Association, 910 Charles Street, Fredericksburg, VA 22401; (540) 368-0590; fax: (540) 370-0015; Web site: www.iherb.org or the Association of Specialty Cut Flower Growers, 155 Elm Street, Oberlin, OH 44074; (440) 774-2887; fax: (440) 774-2435. Appropriate Technology Transfer for Rural Areas (ATTRA), P.O. Box 3657, Fayetteville, AR 72702; (800) 346-9140, has very good packets of free information available on a variety of market gardening topics.

If you're seeking hands-on experience before you start your business, the USDA has compiled a list of "Educational and Training Opportunities in Sustainable Agriculture." Contact the Alternative Farming Systems Information Center, National Agricultural Library, Room 304, 10301 Baltimore Boulevard, Beltsville, MD 20705; (301) 504-6559; fax: (301) 504-6409; e-mail: afsic@nal.usda.gov, for a copy, or visit their Web site: www.nal.usda.gov/afsic.

Made in the Shade

Q: *Part of my garden is under a large tree limb and gets a fair amount of shade. Which vegetables will do OK here?*

A: Some crops, like lettuce, need a shady spot that offers them protection from the hot afternoon sun. Light shade is also is a good place to grow herbs like chervil and parsley and, according to a Rodale classic, *The Basic Book of Organic Gardening* (Rodale, 1971), edited by Robert Rodale, kohlrabi does well in areas without excessive sunlight.

In spring, use the spot to sow your early crops, like peas. You'll be harvesting these by the time your tree leafs out. More of a problem than shade from those leaves, however, is competition for food and water from the tree's roots. Be sure that whatever is growing in your shady garden spot is well fed and gets enough water.

The Slanted Garden

Q: *I have a long, sloping garden (about 8 feet wide × 40 feet long) in which I'd like to grow vegetables. Can you suggest some good combinations and successions that would utilize this space efficiently?*

CHECK IT OUT!

Growing vegetables in a shady yard can be a challenge, but you can still harvest armloads of produce if you plan your garden so that every area makes the best use of the sunlight it receives. Orient your beds and rows to run east-west (the way the sun travels in the sky). Trellis your vining plants (like cucumbers) up into the sunlight by growing them on vertical supports. Just remember to put trellised crops on the north side of the garden so that they don't shade out shorter crops.

A: Wide rows or raised beds running across the slope of the hill (terrace fashion) will keep the soil from washing downward. So will intensive plantings in which the soil remains covered with growing plants at all times, says Sally Cunningham, master gardener and author of *Great Garden Companions: A Companion-Planting System for a Beautiful Chemical-Free Vegetable Garden* (Rodale, 1998).

You could "start with beds of peas, lettuce, and spinach to hold down the soil during spring rains," she says. As the peas finish producing, follow them with warm season vegetables like beans, tomatoes, and peppers. In late spring, "seed cucumbers and melons (or set kohlrabi transplants, for example) among the lettuce while it is still growing," she adds.

As the vine crops get going, seed sweet corn in among the young plants, spacing the corn at least 1 foot apart in all directions. If possible, plant the sweet corn on the south side of the lettuce so that it can shade the lettuce and delay its bolting as the summer gets hot, suggests Cunningham.

Potatoes don't necessarily combine well with other crops (hilling them disturbs the soil around them), but you could border their bed with lettuce, carrots, alyssum, or calendula. Herbs and flowers make good companions for vegetables because they attract beneficial insects that will pollinate your crops or help control pest insects. "Any wide-row vegetable planting can benefit from some herbs and flowers mixed right into the bed or along the outside edge," says Cunningham.

And if you find yourself with undesirable bare beds or unfinished edges throughout the growing season, consider planting a short-term cover crop, such as buckwheat. "It's pretty and quick to cover the ground, it improves the soil, and it can be turned under easily at any time," says Cunningham. For an attractive living mulch that will build up the soil's nitrogen, plant low-growing dwarf white clover around the tomato cages, she adds.

Water Wisdom

Q: *Sometimes when we're watering a thirsty vegetable crop, we end up overwatering a less-thirsty vegetable nearby. What vegetables should we plant together to avoid this problem?*

A: An easy rule to remember when planting your garden that will help you to be "water-wise" is to group plants by how big they'll get and how fast they grow, says Tim Hartz, Ph.D., extension vegetable specialist at the University of California at Davis.

For example, plant lettuce, spinach, radishes, beets, and carrots in the same garden area. They grow at about the same rate and, therefore, need the same amount of water. So do sweet corn, tomatoes, melons, and other crops that grow large rapidly. But these fast and furious growers also need a lot of water, so you'll want to plant them in a designated "high water usage" area of the garden, says Dr. Hartz.

Dr. Hartz also suggests that if you sow successive crops of lettuce, spinach, and so on, you should keep each run together in their own areas based on planting date. That way, you won't have lettuce seedlings at one end of a row and mature plants (with vastly different water requirements) at the other end.

ASPARAGUS

The Cutting Edge

Q: *I'd like to know how late in the summer I can cut asparagus.*

A: Stop picking your asparagus when the diameter of the largest spears drops to less than ⅜ inch, or the size of a pencil. (You can pick all the thin spears you want until it happens; we're saying to stop when you don't see any big spears anymore.) When thick spears get scarce, it means the vigor of the plant is falling off. It needs to grow undisturbed and rest up to give you tasty spears again the following year.

Extending Asparagus

Q: *Can you tell me for how long a time period I can harvest asparagus?*

A: The conventional advice is to harvest asparagus spears for 6 to 10 weeks each spring and then stop cutting so that the plants will develop the ferny top growth that's necessary to replenish carbohydrate stores for the next year's crop. But Cornell University researchers have developed an alternative technique that can extend the harvest period by at least 2 weeks: Harvest as usual for the first 2 weeks. Then select two or three sturdy spears in each crown and leave them uncut while you continue to cut newly appearing spears. These "mother stalks" will stimulate your plants to produce more harvestable spears at the same time they're collecting solar energy to form next year's stalks. Keep the plants well watered and continue harvesting until all the newly emerging spears are thinner than a pencil.

Weeds in Asparagus

Q: *I have a 25-year-old patch of asparagus with a tremendous weed problem. I once tried salt water, but a light solution had no effect, and a strong solution killed the asparagus.*

A: Salt can help control weeds in asparagus, but this method has its limitations. "Salt is only effective against young, germinating seeds; it will not kill established weeds, nor will it provide any lasting effect," says Wade H. Elmer, Ph.D., associate plant pathologist at the Connecticut Agricultural Experiment Station, who has studied the use of rock salt for disease and weed control in asparagus.

"Salt is more effective for retarding the gradual yield decline in asparagus that is caused by crown- and root-rotting diseases," explains Dr. Elmer. If your asparagus is not producing as much as it used to and the ferns are stunted and/or yellow, here's how to use salt most effectively: Start with sodium chloride—a.k.a. rock salt, kosher salt, pickling salt, or ice-melting salt. Once a year in early spring, broadcast 1 pound of salt per 20 feet of row, spreading it 2½ feet out from each side, instructs Dr. Elmer. But don't try this on salt-sensitive plants—you could ruin your garden. Unlike most garden plants, "asparagus likes brackish water; a tidal basin that gets flooded with saltwater once a year is ideal for asparagus," explains Dr. Elmer.

Mulching might be a better weed control method than salt, he says. After you harvest your spears this spring, put down a thick layer of organic mulch (one that's free of seeds!). "Here near the coast, a lot of people use salt hay for mulch, but compost or other organic material also would work," says Dr. Elmer. Once the asparagus crowns go dormant in late fall, you can really pile on the mulch, he adds. But pull it back early next spring so the spears can come up again. For added insurance against crown and root rot, you can spread salt on top of the mulch—water will leach the salt through it.

Make sure whatever mulch you add doesn't change the pH of the soil beneath it. "Asparagus likes a high pH, from 7.0 to 7.5. Monitor the pH with periodic soil tests, and if you find the pH dropping too low, apply lime to the bed in the fall to raise it," he advises.

CHECK IT OUT!

Contrary to popular belief, bigger is better when you're growing asparagus. Give them a taste test and you'll soon discover that thicker spears are more tender than thin spears. That's because both thick and thin spears have a certain number of tough, fibrous strands in them. The smaller the diameter of the spear, the closer the tough fibers are packed together, and the tougher the texture is. Large spears have more room for succulent flesh between the fibers, so they're more tender.

Salt Solution Brings Deer to Asparagus Patch

Q: *After reading an item in Organic Gardening magazine recommending salt as a remedy for fusarium crown rot, I tried it last year and the results were disastrous. The local deer, which had never seemed to like asparagus before, ate the stalks off when they were about 18 inches high. They also ate the soil, scratching grooves and gullies to get at the salt. Many young spears were broken off just by deer trampling through their new "lick." (Incidentally, I also put salt blocks out for them, so the asparagus bed wasn't their only source.) What went wrong?*

A: Unfortunately, your problem has never wandered onto the beds of leading salt-for-asparagus researcher Wade H. Elmer, Ph.D., associate plant pathologist at the Connecticut Agricultural Experiment Station, so he has little advice on how to avoid it. Perhaps you could try watering the salt into the soil right away to make it less evident, he suggests. More important, he says, you might not need to use it if your plants are healthy and productive. (Symptoms of fusarium infection are mid- to late-season yellowing and drying of stalks and smaller, fewer spears in spring.)

To avoid fusarium without using salt, try to eliminate stresses on your plants, such as overharvesting.

BEANS

Beans and Itchy Skin

Q: *We plant several varieties of green beans each year. When I pick them, my skin always becomes* *inflamed and very itchy, lasting for days. Are the bean leaves causing this reaction?*

A: Yes, some people can be allergic to bean plants, says David M. Webster, Ph.D., project leader for pea and bean breeding at Asgrow Seed Company's research facility in Twin Falls, Idaho. "I get an allergic reaction when I work around beans," he says, "but as long as I wear gloves and a long-sleeved shirt, I'm OK." You should already be wearing a long-sleeved shirt to protect your skin from sunshine, he reminds us. Add the gloves and you should be OK for the next harvest.

Bean Inoculants

Q: *I always thought bacterial strains varied widely in their ability to bind nitrogen for specific legumes. What are seed suppliers selling when they offer soil inoculant for all* Phaseolus *cultivars?*

A: "Inoculants for all commercial varieties of *Phaseolus vulgaris*, or common bean, generally contain at least two different strains of nitrogen-fixing *Rhizobium* bacteria," says Marianne Sarrantonio, Ph.D., former legume coordinator at the Rodale Institute Experimental Farm in Maxatawny, Pennsylvania. "The strains from reputable companies have been selected through careful testing to ensure they are most competitive—because the inoculants are competing with rhizobial populations free-living in the soil—and most effective for the widest number of species and varieties.

"*Phaseolus* is notorious for fixing nitrogen poorly even under ideal conditions," Dr. Sarrantonio says. If you're trying to increase the nitrogen in your soil, consider growing cowpeas and nitrogen-fixing cover crops. If you're trying to grow better beans, however, the *Phaseolus* inoculants are generally inexpensive. Follow package instructions, use fresh inoculant, and plant legumes immediately after inoculating the soil. Be sure to build soil health in other ways, too, such as by adding compost and other organic matter and rotating your crops.

Three-Bean Letter

Q: *I'm not sure whether or not to plant beans twice in the same place in my garden, or whether to pull up spent plants and destroy them, or whether to plow them under. Please shed some light on this for me.*

A: Rotating the location of beans in your garden is a good idea, says Matt J. Silbernagel, Ph.D., USDA researcher at Washington State University's Irrigated Agricultural Research and Extension Center in Prosser. "There are few places where you aren't going to get a buildup of root rot and foliar disease if you grow beans on beans," he says. (Bean root rots and virus diseases are more of a problem west of the Rockies, while foliar diseases such as halo blight, anthracnose, and rust are more common in the East, he adds.)

There is an advantage to planting beans in the same place. The rhizobium bacteria (that take nitrogen from the air and feed it to your plants) that they harbor will keep building up in the soil and you wouldn't have to inoculate your bean seeds each year to ensure that the plants get enough nitrogen. But, you do risk disease, which is probably not a good trade-off.

Many bean lovers report good results when they split the difference by using the same patch for beans every other year. They tell us that they don't have to re-inoculate because the beans get plenty of nitrogen and disease is kept at bay.

Finally, turning under your bean debris might be effective if you live in the East and the dead plants can decompose completely in the soil.

Baby Vegetables

Q: *My broccoli and cauliflower plants showed vigorous growth early on and developed huge leaves, but the heads stayed small. I enrich the soil each year with packaged, composted cow manure. Could the nutrient balance be off?*

A: These plants will produce small heads if they're exposed to really cold temperatures in the seedling stage, says David Wolfe, Ph.D., associate professor of plant science at Cornell University. Did you set them out extra early? Did they get snowed on?

Other stresses that can keep the heads of these brassicas undersize include drought at a critical time in head development, insect damage, or setting out transplants that are too large or too old. Dr. Wolfe recommends that only small, hardy transplants with no more than four or five true leaves be used for spring planting. And yes, overfertilization—especially with nitrogen (as in cow manure)—can keep heads small, so have your soil tested before you add any more manure.

Broccoli Sprouts Fight Cancer

Q: *I recently read that broccoli sprouts contained 20 to 50 times more sulforaphane, a cancer fighter, than mature broccoli heads. Can I grow broccoli sprouts from seed purchased at my local lawn and garden store? Any suggestions on growing these sprouts?*

A: First, a warning: Use only untreated seeds to grow edible sprouts. Some seeds have been treated with fungicides to improve their germination in cold or disease-infested soils. Some treated seeds are dyed pink; some aren't. You don't want to eat those chemicals. (You don't even want them in your garden—they're prohibited in a certified organic growing system.)

That said, you can use untreated broccoli seeds of any variety to grow your own broccoli sprouts. One source of untreated broccoli seeds is Johnny's Selected Seeds in Albion, Maine (see "Resources" on page 234). They also sell sprouters, or you can make your own with a sterilized wide-mouthed quart jar and a piece of cheesecloth or nylon mesh. Thoroughly rinse about 3 tablespoons of the seeds in water, then soak them for 6 to 8 hours. The duds will float to the surface; skim them off. Next, put the seeds in the jar along with some tepid water. Secure the fabric over the opening with a canning ring or rubber band, drain the seeds thoroughly, then prop up the jar on a slant so that it can continue to drain. Average household temperatures are fine.

Continue to rinse and drain the seeds at least twice a day to prevent mold from growing. As soon as the sprouts appear, move the jar into bright light (but not direct sunlight) to green them up. Researchers at Johns Hopkins University found the high levels of protective compounds in broccoli sprouts that were 3 days old.

Also, you might want to try growing your own seeds. Start some plants indoors about 4 or 5 weeks before you'd normally plant peas outside, instructs Rob Johnston, president of Johnny's. Transplant the seedlings outside while it's still cold. "That will usually induce bolting," he comments. Since you're growing these plants for seed instead of for the edible heads, you can space them as close as 8 inches apart. (Figure on getting about ⅓ pound of broccoli seed per square foot of growing space.) After the flowering stage, when the masses of seedpods turn brown, clip plants at the base, and put them under cover to dry. To separate the seeds from the pods, stuff whole plants into a cloth bag, and step on it firmly enough to release the seeds, but lightly enough to avoid damaging them. Then use a window fan to blow away the debris, suggests Johnston.

CABBAGE

Turning Heads

Q: *My husband loves Chinese cabbage so we ordered seeds and grew some in containers. They were green and healthy-looking but never developed heads. I ordered more seeds, specifically the Napa types, but no luck either. Is there a secret to making these things look like Chinese cabbage?*

A: Some Chinese cabbages don't form a solid head but grow into a more loose-leaf shape. "My first suspicion is that these Napas are a nonheading type," says Vincent Rubatzky, Ph.D., extension vegetable specialist at the University of California. Did you actually see a picture of the cabbage in the seed catalog or on the packet?

Were they crowded in the container? "If plants are very closely spaced, heading may be delayed," says Dr. Rubatzky. Overwatering or overfertilization can also hinder heading. (Compost should provide enough food.)

And when did you try to grow them? Varieties vary in their heat tolerance; some are better suited for spring crops and some do better in the fall. Hot temperatures interfere with heading, says Dr. Rubatzky. Early spring or late fall is no bargain either—exposure to cold temperatures can cause the plant to go to seed without forming a solid head, adds Douglas Sanders, Ph.D., extension specialist at North Carolina State University.

Disappearing Cabbage

Q: *Please tell me what happened to my cabbage plants. Each time I set out transplants, they disappeared completely within 4 days. I found no worms or animal tracks.*

A: It's possible that your pests are nocturnal. Slugs, cutworms, and the like do their damage at night, so get out your flashlight because the first thing you have to do is identify what's chomping on your cabbages, says Burton R. Evans, Ph.D., extension entomologist at the University of Georgia.

Cutworm larvae are 1 to 2 inches long and grayish or brown. Try hand-picking them or protecting young plants with collars made from tin cans or cardboard tubes sunk a few inches into the soil. They are caterpillars (*Lepidoptera*), so BT (*Bacillus thuringiensis*), a naturally occurring bacterium that's only toxic to caterpillars, sprayed on your plants will kill them after they take a bite. Cutworm larvae are also a favorite food of birds, so cultivate your soil a few times prior to setting out your next run of plants to expose them to your feathered friends.

If you find slugs, handpick them at night, or sink beer traps at soil level near your plants. Change the beer daily, Dr. Evans says. "It gets foul pretty quickly." You can also try putting down boards between plant rows and scraping the slugs off the bottoms first thing in the morning. Wood ashes and diatomaceous earth are good barriers against snails and slugs until they get damp, Dr. Evans adds.

Tiny Green Worms

Q: *Last year, I started cabbage plants from seed. While the plants were still indoors, I noticed small ragged holes in the leaves and found small green caterpillars on the undersides of the leaves. I had* *started the seeds in new flats and used a commercial bagged seed starting mix—where did those little worms come from?!*

A: Those little green worms most likely hatched out of eggs that were laid on your cabbage plants by an adult female moth that somehow got into your house. (Moths are attracted to light and open doors.) There are quite a few kinds of similar-looking cabbage pests, including the cabbage loopers, army-worms, and the caterpillars of diamondback moths.

If you find those little green worms on your young cabbage plants again this year while they're still indoors, pick them off by hand. If worms start showing up on your plants once you transplant them outside, however, more serious action is in order. Spray the plants with a solution of BTK—*Bacillus thuringiensis* var. *kurstaki*, a naturally occurring bacterium that's toxic to caterpillars and nothing else. You can buy BT products in garden centers (some brand names include Dipel, MVP, Javelin, and Safer), or you can order them from almost any seed catalog. Make sure the product contains the correct strain (*kurstaki*) of BT for use against caterpillar pests (other types work against Colorado potato beetles and mosquito larvae). Spray the plants thoroughly, covering both top and bottom of the leaves as the caterpillars must eat BT-sprayed leaves before they'll die. They won't die immediately—the BT takes a couple of days to finish them off—but they'll stop eating your cabbages right away.

Little Red Cabbage

Q: *I've grown green cabbages for years with good results, but when I try to grow red cabbages, they either do not form heads at all or form only very small ones. For example, when I grew one variety in both spring and fall, the heads weighed only 1 to 2 pounds instead* *of the 3 pounds promised in the catalog. 'Red Salad De-light' does not seem to be available anymore. Does red cabbage require different soil nutrients than green? Is there a red cabbage variety that will grow large?*

A: Red cabbages typically form smaller heads than their green cousins because of the anthocyanin in their leaves. "This is the compound that results in the red color, but red leaves are not able to accumulate as much light as the green, so photosynthesis is decreased," explains Wolfgang Bauch, plant breeder for Seminis Vegetable Seeds in Woodland, California. You can compensate for this and help red cabbages grow larger by adding a little more nitrogen to their soil, he advises. One way to do this would be to mix some aged, composted manure into the soil a couple of weeks before planting.

Even so, heads on early maturing varieties (50 days to maturity from transplant) usually average only about 2 pounds, Bauch says. "You could get heavier heads if you plant very early in the spring, but if you grow the crop in the fall, when the days are getting shorter and the light is lessening, the heads will be smaller. We recommend early varieties for spring growing or for areas that have only a very short growing season, but not for fall growing," he states.

Some varieties of red cabbage can grow larger, however. Varieties that require a longer growing season (75 to 85 days) can be expected to produce heads weighing 4 to 6 pounds. (Check catalog descriptions to determine which varieties will work best for you.) To get heads that size, you need long, bright days with temperatures in the 60s. Next year, try setting out transplants of a later-maturing red cabbage about 1 month before your last frost in soil that is a little richer than normal; then hope for a long, cool spring. Hot temperatures can prevent cabbage, both red and green, from forming solid heads.

Woody Carrot Core

Q: *How can I eliminate the dark, dense, woody core I keep getting in my carrots? The core is dark brown except for the upper end, where it's bright green. (I grow my carrots in a solar greenhouse; the original soil was heavy with caliche but now has lots of organic matter.)*

A: The evidence suggests that you're growing an older carrot variety, that you're underwatering, and that you're waiting too long to harvest, theorizes Robert Maxwell, Ph.D., a plant breeder for Peto Sluis Seed Company.

To begin with, try growing a newer, hybrid variety that has been specifically bred not to turn green or get tough, he suggests. "A lot of the Nantes varieties [both hybrid and open-pollinated] fit this definition, as do the newer Imperator types," he explains. As for your treelike core, carrots turn woody this way as they get old and ready to bolt (send up their flowerstalks and set seeds in the second year of their life) or if they don't get enough water. "So prevent your woody problem by harvesting your carrots young and keeping them moist, especially at harvesttime," says Dr. Maxwell. Follow his advice, he explains, and your carrots "will be crisper with better flavor and a nicer texture."

Rubber Carrots

Q: *Why do my carrots, even with refrigeration, turn to rubber within hours of being harvested, while store-bought ones stay crisp for weeks?*

A: Are you storing your homegrown carrots like store-bought ones? That is, in a perforated, but closed plastic bag in your refrigerator's vegetable drawer? If not, the carrots' humidity level may not be high enough, says Helen Harrison, Ph.D., horticulture professor at the University of Wisconsin, where carrot research is a priority.

If you have a vegetable drawer with a humidity control, set it at the highest possible level to keep your carrots crisp, says Dr. Harrison. Only mature carrots will store well—and only if you cut off all but 1 inch of their leaves first. Don't even try to store young, immature carrots—eat them immediately instead.

Underachieving Carrots

Q: *We used to grow 'Sweetness' carrots that were up to 21 inches long. But the last few years, as soon as our carrots get to "baby size," the leafy tops start turning black. Soon the whole crop has this plague and growth stops. What can we do about it?*

A: The problem could be Alternaria leaf blight and the disease could be seedborne, says James Strandberg, Ph.D., professor of plant pathology at the University of Florida, who specializes in carrot diseases. "If you keep trying to grow infected seed from year to year, the problem will continue," he warns. "The best thing to do is to try another source of seeds." Also, if your garden is surrounded by fields of wild carrots (Queen-Anne's-lace), they could be transmitting the disease to your carrots. To get rid of the wild ones, mow them down before they can flower and set their seeds.

And grow your carrots in another part of the garden. Alternaria, as well as black rot (another carrot disease), can overwinter on the remains of the plants, says Dr. Strandberg. If you can't rotate your carrot crop to another location, be sure to clean up and destroy all carrot debris at the end of the season. And plant your new carrots where they'll get full sun, and thin them out so they have lots of air space around their tops to help their foliage dry quickly, he adds.

Wants 'Em Sweeter

Q: *I've been growing many carrots varieties for years and, although they look great, they're often bitter and never as sweet as store-bought carrots. They have some root hairs but not an excessive amount, and I have no problem with forking. I am wondering if too much nitrogen could be the problem. I amend the soil before planting with compost and sand (the soil here has a lot of clay in it). What about pH? I want to grow sweet carrots. Any suggestions?*

A: First, are your carrots under stress? Alternating periods of too much or too little water can make for a bitter harvest, as could extreme heat or other stress, says Helen Harrison, Ph.D., horticulture professor at the University of Wisconsin. Dr. Harrison adds that too much nitrogen won't cause a bitter flavor (although it could give you more leaves than roots) and that carrots grow best in a soil with a pH of 6.0 to 7.0.

Are you trying to produce sweet carrots at the height of the hot summer? Warm (not hot) days, cool nights, and moderate soil temperatures are the best conditions for great-tasting carrots, says master muncher Rob Johnston of Johnny's Selected Seeds in Albion, Maine. If you grow carrots in the spring, plant a fast-maturing variety and plant early, so the carrots can mature before it gets too hot, says Wayne J. McLaurin, Ph.D., horticulturist at the University of Georgia.

Dr. McLaurin (who prefers to grow his carrots as a fall crop that he overwinters with a little protection) also suggests you try growing a Nantes-type carrot (which matures a little earlier than other types) or baby carrots.

CORN

Awful Corn Problem

Q: *I have an awful corn problem. I planted supersweet 'Zenith' last year and 'Silver Queen' this year, and both had the same problems: 1) stunted, misshapen ears, most with just a few plump kernels near the bottom and one side of the ear; 2) huge, ghastly, deformed bluish "kernels" that don't seem to match the descriptions of corn smut I have seen (they are inside the husk); and 3) ants everywhere—on and in the developing ears (are they a problem, or just an annoyance?). What could be wrong?*

A: Terry Kelley, Ph.D., extension vegetable horticulturist at the Rural Development Center in Tifton, Georgia, thinks your misshapen, poorly filled ears are a pollination problem. Did you plant your corn very late, he asks? If you plant too late, hot weather will make good pollination difficult to achieve. Also, 'Silver Queen' needs more time to ripen than almost any other corn you might choose to grow. You might have better luck with any faster-maturing variety.

Yes, the horror you describe is corn smut. This fungal infection develops inside the husk and explodes to the outside (which is when most people notice it). Corn smut thrives in hot weather, says Dr. Kelley, and its presence is another indication that you may be planting your corn too late. To lessen the chance that you'll see smut, be sure you plant as early as possible, rotate your corn plantings, and destroy infected ears by burning them. (Don't compost them; the fungus would probably thrive in your pile.)

Wayne J. McLaurin, Ph.D., extension horticulturist with the University of Georgia, says that the ants on your corn are probably seeking aphid droppings, their preferred food. And those aphids can also interfere with pollination if a lot of them are present at the silking and tasseling stage. Beneficials such as ladybugs and lacewings will feed on the aphids; having some pollen and nectar plants like dill or fennel in bloom nearby will attract these plant-protecting beneficials.

Dr. McLaurin also wondered how your corn has been planted. Best pollination takes place when corn is planted in blocks of short rows, not in one long row. Dr. McLaurin also believes that a lack of soil fertility could contribute to the kind of poor "kernel fill" you describe. Next time, feed your stalks with a high-nitrogen fertilizer every week or so and keep your plants well watered. Corn will remove nitrogen from the soil at the rate of 140 pounds per acre; this means that for every 100 square feet of corn, you should add a total of 3½ pounds of bloodmeal (which contains about 10 percent nitrogen) or about 35 pounds of compost (1 percent nitrogen) to the soil over the growing season.

The third expert we consulted, Randy Hudson, extension entomologist with the University of Georgia, suspects stinkbugs. "It's not uncommon to have the symptoms you've described if stinkbugs feed on the developing ear after the corn has begun to silk," he says. Stinkbugs have piercing mouthparts; as they suck on plants, they also inject an enzyme. "The enzyme and the removal of plant juices both can cause corn ears to develop abnormally," says Hudson.

You can handpick stinkbugs if your corn patch isn't too large. They will be most active during the warmer, sunnier parts of the day, says Hudson. "But the best recommendation," he says, "is to time your crops so that the stinkbugs aren't looking for a new home just when your corn is tasseling." (Stinkbugs will move into your corn about the time any greens you had planted the previous fall—overwintered kale, collards, or mustards, for instance—succumb to warm spring temperatures.)

Is your corn patch next to a grainfield? Stinkbugs will move out of there, too, when the grain matures (as leaves and stems turn brown, they get too tough for the stinkbugs to eat). Again, this can occur right about the time that corn is tasseling. Hudson also says to plant early and maybe plant a "trap crop": Surround your corn patch with a few rows of earlier-maturing corn to protect your main crop in the center.

Crammed Corn

Q: *I am a true sweet corn nut, but I live on a small, suburban lot and don't have the room to space anything 9 inches apart in rows 30 inches apart. Can I cram more corn into a smaller space? Should I use raised beds?*

A: Yes. We consulted the bible of garden cramming, *How to Grow More Vegetables Than You Ever Thought Possible on Less Land Than You Can Imagine* (Ten Speed Press, 1991), and then called the cramming expert who wrote it, John Jeavons. This longtime proponent of double-dug, raised-bed, biointensive gardening says that by planting sweet corn seeds 15 inches apart in all directions (on 15-inch centers instead of rows) you can grow lots of plants in a small area—provided you enjoy very fertile, deep soil.

Jeavons has a couple more suggestions for getting the most corn out of the least space. Choose a variety with proven high yields, he says, and germinate the seeds in flats or little biodegradable containers (peat or newspaper pots, etc.) about a week before you're ready to set them into the garden. Plant them pot and all. "If you wait longer, it doesn't work very well because of how the root system grows," he says. The advantage of using transplants, he explains, is that you won't worry about spotty germination ruining your tight-space plans. "You know you have a living plant at each point; and you can choose the most vigorous of your transplants as well."

You can grow smaller corn plants even closer together. 'Orchard Baby' sweet corn grows only 3 to 5 feet tall, but it will still produce two or three 4- to 6-inch-long ears per plant. It can be spaced as close as 12 inches apart. "It is very good yielding and grows well in cool weather," says Jeavons, "so you can start it at least a month earlier than other corn." 'Orchard Baby' is available from Bountiful Gardens in Willits, California (see "Resources" on page 234).

Sparse Kernels

Q: *For the past 3 years, most of my corn has filled in poorly on short, stubby ears that have a slight curl to the tips. It certainly doesn't look like the pictures on the seed packets. What can I do?*

A: Sister Mary Francis Heimann, plant disease diagnostician at the University of Wisconsin, says that the slight curl to the tips of the ears could indicate a phosphorus deficiency. She recommends you have your soil tested. She also adds that if weather and soil are too dry at tasseling time, the pollen won't fertilize the ears properly. "First, have your soil tested," she advises. And if your soil is fine but your summers have been dry, try watering at tasseling time.

Gerald Pataky, Ph.D., plant pathologist at the University of Illinois, says that two bacterial diseases—Stewart's wilt and Goss's wilt—result in small ears with sparse kernels. The Stewart's wilt bacteria overwinters in flea beetles and is thus spread from one year to the next. The Goss's wilt bacteria enters the plant after it has been damaged by insects, hail, or some other physical force.

Dr. Pataky believes the best defense against the wilts is to plant resistant varieties. If a variety is resistant to Stewart's wilt, it's probably resistant to Goss's as well. Some seed companies are especially good about telling you which of their varieties have resistance.

Segregating Corn

Q: *An article in* Organic Gardening *magazine said to plant popcorn at least 50 feet away from sweet corn, but I've also read that you should plant popcorn at least 100 to 150 feet away from supersweet corns because if they cross-pollinate, the supersweet will be tough. Which is correct?*

A: Depends on whom you talk to and what you're trying to achieve. The most important thing to remember is that corn with the supersweet gene (also called sh2 corn) must be isolated from other corns to protect the crop. If sh2 corn cross-pollinates with non-sh2, its sweetness will be lost and you'll get tough, bland kernels on your supersweet stalks. Similarly, popcorn, other sweet corns, and field corns should also be separated. If the period when these crops pollinate overlaps, their pollen could mix and produce tough/starchy corn instead of sweet juicy kernels.

How far you need to separate a supersweet from another type of corn is influenced by a number of factors and is the subject of widely differing opinions. Mike Orzolek, Ph.D., professor of vegetable crops at Penn State University, says that a distance of 500 feet is necessary to really prevent another corn's pollen from reaching your supersweet, but depending on terrain and wind direction, you may be able to plant closer. A patch of tall sunflowers or some other type of windbreak also keeps pollen from traveling. Some experts believe that 25 feet is far enough, some say 50 feet, while others insist on 100 feet, etc. (You tell us a distance, we'll find an expert who says that's the minimum.)

If you time your plantings so that your corns don't tassel and release their pollen at the same time, you can grow supersweet corn close to another type without worrying about the distance factor. Just be sure they reach their pollen

Gardeners have long tried to control ear worms by applying a few drops of vegetable oil to the tip of each corn ear. Recently, researchers have found that adding BTK (Bacillus thuringiensis var. kurstaki, a naturally occurring bacteria) to the oil helped prevent almost all of the damage usually caused by the worms. Just mix 1 part diluted BTK to 20 parts vegetable oil. Then apply three to five drops of the BTK/oil mixture at the tip of each ear, just as the silks begin to turn brown.

stage at least 14 days apart. For example, Dr. Orzolek says, if you want to grow a 72-day supersweet corn, you can grow it near any nonsupersweet type that matures about 14 days earlier or later (if you plant them on the same day).

If you want to save seed to grow the same variety of corn again, you need to isolate all types and varieties. You can either plant your varieties far apart, time their pollinations carefully, or hand-pollinate as follows (as recommended by the Seed Savers Exchange in Decorah, Iowa):

Cut off the tips of ears (husks and silks, not cobs) just before the silks emerge to ensure no unwanted pollen reaches them. Immediately place a bag over each ear, then bag the tassels to collect the pollen. Staple the bags in place. In a short time, you'll have enough pollen to sprinkle on the silks, which will have grown 1 inch or so beyond the tip of the trimmed ear. To ensure good genetics, mix all the pollen in one bag before applying it to the silks. Remove the ear bags, dust the pollen on the silks, then reseal the ear in the bag.

Corn Quiz

Q: *What is the function of corn silk? And is corn fattening? I know it's given to animals to fatten them up, and I try to eat a fat-free diet.*

A: Corn silk is a long hollow tube through which the pollen from the corn flower (the tassel that forms on the top of the plants) travels to reach the seeds (those kernels we love to later eat) to pollinate them.

Although corn does contain enough vegetable oil that it is considered worthwhile to grow as an "oil crop," it is nonetheless not fattening. One ear of corn averages 83 calories, 11 percent of which come from a single gram of mostly polyunsaturated fat. To put that in perspective, the lowest level of fat considered safe for humans to eat is 10 percent of calories—below that you run the risk of becoming deficient in vital nutrients that are contained only in fats.

EGGPLANT
Soft-Boiled Eggplant

Q: *The first time I tried growing eggplants in a container, the plant produced one fruit at a time and the end of the fruit farthest from the stem was very soft. Any ideas why this occurred? Also, the plants only produced one flower at a time, so I used the male flower of a squash for pollination. Did I do the right thing?*

A: Eggplants need a steady, even supply of water, says Francis "Frank" Ferrandino, Ph.D., associate scientist at the Connecticut Agricultural Experiment Station; and plants grown outdoors in containers can dry out very quickly (especially if the container is one that "wicks" moisture, like terra-cotta). The soft spot you describe at the end of the fruit can occur if the rapidly growing cells in that portion of the plant don't get enough water and die, he adds.

The next time you grow an eggplant in captivity, do it in a big nonporous pot. "The container needs to be large enough so that the soil can stay moist on a hot summer day," explains Dr. Ferrandino—that's at least 2 gallons in size. Fill that container with a heavy (moisture-retaining) potting soil, and mulch the top with compost or another organic material to help keep the moisture from evaporating.

Also, "make sure you plant an eggplant variety that bears small fruit," emphasizes Dr. Ferrandino. Avoid varieties described as "vigorous" and "spreading"; some can grow up to

4 feet tall—with proportionately large (and thirsty) root systems. Read seed catalog descriptions carefully and choose a variety like 'Early Black Egg', whose 2-foot plants produce nice little 6-inch fruits in just 70 days. (Seeds for 'Early Black Egg' are available from Garden City Seeds in Hamilton, Montana, and from Southern Exposure Seed Exchange in Earlysville, Virginia—see "Resources" on page 234.)

And don't worry about pollination—eggplant flowers are "self-fertile" and don't need pollen from another flower in order to bear fruit. In addition, squash and eggplant are unrelated (squash belongs to the Cucurbit family, while eggplant is a Solanaceae), so the squash pollen you dusted onto the eggplant flower had no effect whatsoever.

Unproductive Eggplant

Q: *Why do my eggplants refuse to bear fruit?*

A: "Eggplant is notoriously an inconsistent performer in this area," says Richard Ashley, Ph.D., extension vegetable crops specialist at the University of Connecticut. "Two factors contribute to your fruitless eggplants: climate and soil nutrient levels."

The first flush of eggplant blossoms to appear do not set fruit, probably because of cool night temperatures or wet weather. The plants grow vegetation vigorously, and by the time the second flush of flowers appears, it's too late in the growing season for the fruit to develop fully. Also, using compost or manure every year may build up nutrient levels so the plants become overfed.

Dr. Ashley recommends reducing fertilizer levels to limit vegetative growth. When the first blossoms drop, cultivate 4 to 5 inches deep with a rotary tiller next to plants to prune roots and shock the plants out of the vegetation phase. If the eggplants are in rows, till along either side of the row. If planted on the square, till only along two sides of the plant. University researchers have also experimented with row covers, but with little success.

"Many commercial growers will plant two or three varieties of eggplant, hoping one variety will set fruit," Dr. Ashley says. The standard among many of those growers is 'Classic'. Try 'Ichiban', which he says bears a bit more consistently than others.

GARLIC
Turning Blue over Green Garlic

Q: *Each year I grow a lot of garlic. I followed a recipe for pickling garlic, but the garlic now appears to be turning a greenish color. Is it safe to eat?*

A: Yes, it is. It's not uncommon for pickled garlic to turn green—or blue. Don't worry! But both colors are safe to eat.

Leslie Norris, a food chemist at McCormick & Company, explains that the bluish or greenish color is caused by a naturally occurring enzymatic reaction. When the clove is damaged or cut in any way (including small cuts from peeling), an enzyme is released and the reaction begins. And refrigerating the garlic in oil encourages this color-changing activity. The reaction doesn't affect the quality or flavor of the garlic.

For those of you who want to make some naturally blue/green garlic, here's our recipe: Peel the garlic cloves, put them in a glass container, cover them with vinegar, then cover the container, and let it sit for at least 24 hours. Drain the garlic-flavored vinegar from the cloves, and use the vinegar in a recipe. Put the cloves in a clean jar, and cover them with any kind of oil—olive oil is an especially good choice. You can store that jar in the refrigerator for up to 5 months, fishing out cloves whenever you need some garlic. When the jar finally becomes clove-free, use the garlic-flavored oil for stir-fries and salads.

Hotter Garlic

Q: *Is there a variety of garlic that's hotter than other garlics? If so, where can I get some to plant?*

A: If you want to torture your garlic into hotness, deny it water, don't mulch it, and/or plant it in soil that's low in organic matter and nutrients. "Poor soil and stress tend to produce hotter garlic," says Ron Engeland, owner of Filaree Farm, a seed garlic supplier in Okanogan, Washington, adding that "we also think that cold winters tend to make some garlic varieties hotter."

So the same type of garlic can vary in hotness from year to year. But variety does count as well. "Porcelain" garlics have hard necks, smooth paper-white bulbs with tight wrappers, and eight or fewer large cloves per bulb. They like a deep, soft, rich soil, and they need a good cold winter, stresses Engeland.

First, you have to find a variety that will grow and store well in your conditions, suggests Engeland. Go ahead and plant a porcelain type, but—at least the first year—grow a rocambole or an artichoke garlic as well, and try not feeding and/or watering them as much as we generally suggest.

Spotty Garlic

Q: *I grew German extra-hardy garlic successfully for years, but my last crop was about one-third ruined by a type of brown rot that ranged from small*

spots to destruction of whole cloves. Do you have any information on this?

A: Your garlic most likely was affected by *Fusarium oxysporum*, a fungus that causes trouble for garlic growers everywhere. Also known as basal rot, this disease reduces the number of roots that come out of the bottom of the garlic bulb, so you end up with smaller bulbs as well, says David Stern, director of the Garlic Seed Foundation in Rose, New York, an "informal organization of growers and eaters of *Allium sativum.*"

Your first line of defense is to plant only noninfected cloves (ones that are free of those brown spots). *Note:* A single bulb can contain both infected and noninfected cloves, says Stern, so don't assume you can't plant anything from this year's crop (or that an entire bulb is safe because one clove is clean).

If all your garlic has brown spots, buy new planting stock from a reputable source, and use the brown-spotted cloves in spaghetti sauce or another garlicky dish because "they're still fine to eat," says Stern. Plant the "clean" cloves carefully—without cutting or bruising them—in a sunny, well-drained spot where garlic (or any of its allium relatives like onions, chives, shallots, etc.) hasn't grown for at least 7 years.

LETTUCE
Melting Iceberg Lettuce

Q: *I have no luck growing iceberg lettuce. The transplants grow about 1 foot tall after I set them out under row covers, then they seem to rot from within, turning to brown mush.*

A: Sounds like a soilborne fungus is infecting your lettuce, says Robert L. Wick, Ph.D., plant pathologist at the

University of Massachusetts. Lettuce is susceptible to three common fungal diseases: botrytis, rhizoctonia, and sclerotinia. It's difficult to say which specific one is the cause of your problem, but "crop rotation is the key to preventing any type of lettuce fungus," says Dr. Wick.

"Plant your next lettuce crop on well-drained soil that does not have a history of this problem," he advises. If your entire garden is affected (many crops can be infected by these pathogens, not just lettuces), you might have to prepare a new spot for your future lettuce.

"Head lettuce is particularly sensitive to bottom rot because the bottom leaves hang down onto the soil," adds Julie Rawson, organic farmer and talented coordinator of the Northeast Organic Farming Association annual summer conference. "Raised beds help lift the leaves up off the soil a little," she continues, adding that you should be sure to provide adequate spacing. "And the earlier in the season you plant and harvest, the better. Bottom rot sets in quickly in the summertime," she says.

LIMA BEANS

Where Are the Butter Beans?

Q: *A friend and I had a spirited discussion about butter beans. My friend claims that butter beans are really lima beans, but I disagree. Who's right? Also, can you tell me where I can find dried butter beans for eating and for planting?*

A: "Butter bean" is a loose and somewhat regional term for certain kinds of lima beans that are eaten dried instead of fresh as most limas are. Linda Harris, horticulturist with

Ferry-Morse Seeds in Fulton, Kentucky, explains that in the South, dried lima beans, such as 'Jackson Wonder' and 'Florida Speckled', (which produce ½-inch-long tan beans with maroon splotches) are called butter beans because they're usually cooked until they're soft and creamy—"like butter." Even though the uncooked beans don't look like typical lima beans, they're considered lima bean varieties: "And when you cook the dried beans, their purple color fades to green," says Harris.

In fact, the butter beans you're most likely to find in a grocery store are sometimes labeled "large white limas." Francis Giudici, president of L.A. Hearne Co., a bean marketing outfit in King City, California, explains that these butter beans are grown mostly in California, where the climate is dry and the season is long. (They need about 120 days to ripen.)

You can order seeds of butter beans from Southern Exposure Seed Exchange, Vermont Bean Seed Company, and Ferry-Morse Seeds (see "Resources" on page 234).

ONIONS

Bigger Onions, Please!

Q: *We can't seem to grow onions larger than 2 inches in diameter. We have sandy soil and after a soil test, we amended it with lime and well-rotted cow manure. We also grow rye cover crops. We have never been able to grow onions from seed, nor have we been able to grow them from purchased transplants. The only time we get onions is when we plant dry sets, but they're small. We set them out about May 1 and harvest in the beginning of September.*

A: Onion sets *are* the easiest, no-fail way to grow onions, but the varieties used for sets are usually storage onions, and they don't normally get much bigger than 2 inches across. If you want bigger onions, you'll have to grow them from transplants or seeds.

It sounds like your previous failures may be due to your sandy soil not being moist enough. Have you been giving your onions extra water when the skies don't cooperate? Even in a loamy soil, onions need a good inch of water each week (which doesn't *sound* like a lot of water, but it is).

To improve your soil's water-holding qualities, increase the organic matter content by adding lots of compost. (This will add nutrients, too.) Although you've amended your sandy soil with composted manure, it still can't hold moisture or nutrients as well as other soil types. And onions need healthy amounts of readily available food *and* water to grow large.

You've also got to select the right onion variety for your region and season. In Michigan, for example, a "long-day" variety onion does best growing in the long daylight hours in late spring. "Try 'Yellow Sweet Spanish' transplants," suggests Bernard Zandstra, Ph.D., vegetable specialist at Michigan State University. "Select large, healthy transplants, get them in the ground as soon as possible in the spring, and keep them well fertilized and watered," he urges. You should be able to buy transplants of this variety locally from onion farmers or garden shops in your area.

And finally, *don't* wait until May 1 to plant your onions! You're missing out on precious weeks of your onion growing season. Dr. Zandstra says you want your onion tops to be as large as possible before the long days of early June trigger the bulbs to enlarge. Try getting your onions in the ground a month earlier, or as soon as you can work your soil. Don't worry; "most onion plants are pretty hardy and a light frost won't bother them at all," says Dr. Zandstra.

Seeing Double

Q: *Many of our onions form double bulbs, which fail to keep well. We discard them if we are unable to use them quickly. We plant onions each year in early spring from 'Stuttgarter' sets and find them to be excellent keepers, except for those that form double bulbs. What's causing this problem? Should we try another variety?*

A: Stressful growing conditions—anything that keeps onions from expanding—can favor double bulbs, says Mike Orzolek, Ph.D., professor of vegetable crops at Penn State University. He explains that onions really love water, and if they dry out too much, a double bulb could result. One way to guard against this is to mulch your onions with straw, grass clippings, or other organic material to retain more moisture.

And yes, certain varieties are more prone to double bulbs than others, adds Dr. Orzolek. If you want to experiment with other good storage varieties, he recommends that you try 'Yellow Ebenezer'. Eileen Weinsteiger, garden project leader at the Rodale Institute Experimental Farm in Maxatawny, Pennsylvania, likes 'Early Yellow Globe', 'Southport Red Globe', 'Southport White Globe', and 'Yellow Ebenezer'.

Onion Neck Rot

Q: *How can I keep my onions from rotting at the neck in storage?*

A: "Neck rot in storage can be caused either by botrytis fungus or bacteria," says Leonard Pike, Ph.D., professor of horticulture at Texas A&M University and breeder of 'Texas Grano 1015' onion. Although improper storage is frequently blamed, "both diseases are initiated prior to storage. Most neck rot is caused by excessive rain or irrigation within 2 weeks of maturity."

To avoid neck rot, harvest onions when tops just start to fall over, before they've turned brown, says Dr. Pike. Don't water onions within 2 weeks of harvest. Dr. Pike suggests you harvest early if a rainy period is expected. "In the South, where we have periods of heavy rain throughout the summer, commercial onion growers often harvest early, when the tops are still erect."

After harvesting the onions, clip the tops to within 1 inch of the bulbs. Spread the bulbs in a single layer on cardboard or wooden slats, or hang them in a mesh bag in a well-ventilated place, such as a garage. It's important that bulbs dry quickly, says Dr. Pike. He advises drying them in front of a fan for about 4 or 5 days.

Store the bulbs on cardboard or in a mesh bag in a dry location, with temperatures just above freezing. Keeping onions directly on concrete tends to promote decay because moisture builds up beneath the bulbs, he says. Onions tend to sprout at 55° to 60°F, which is the worst range for storing onions, according to Dr. Pike. With proper harvest and storage, most onion varieties will keep for 4 to 5 months.

PEAS

Dead Peas

Q: *What causes peas to yellow and die just before they're ripe?*

A: Diseases such as fusarium wilt (a rare condition in these days of wilt-resistant varieties) can make peas turn yellow and die, but hot weather is more likely to kill the plants before they can produce a full crop. Peas love cooler temperatures, preferably 55° to 75°F. They won't grow well in the heat.

To solve the problem, plant earlier—anytime from 4 to 6 weeks before last frost, and no later than 2 to 3 weeks after frost. (And if it's a fall harvest that's affected, plant later—no earlier than 12 weeks before expected frost.)

To avoid stressing peas, give them ½ to 1 inch of water each week, especially during the critical periods of flowering, seed enlargement, and pod development. Peas require only one application of compost or other slow-acting general fertilizer in spring, but they enjoy a boost (by foliar feeding liquid seaweed extract) two or three times during the growing season.

Pea-Picking Plea

Q: *Last summer we harvested 12 pounds of peas (that's the shelled weight—without the pods), and it took forever to shell them. Can you recommend a mechanical pea sheller for home use so that I don't have to shell all those peas by hand next time? Please help—we planted the same amount of peas this year.*

A: Of course we can direct you to pea shellers; just check out the Lehman's catalog. Thumbing through these pages is like visiting a big old country store filled with every type of equipment and tool for the kitchen, garden, farm, homestead, and nonelectric household. (Many of Lehman's customers are Amish farmers who choose not to use electricity.)

Lehman's "Texas Pea Sheller" could be exactly what you're looking for. It will shell peas or beans and it is hand-powered, but the catalog adds that you can motorize it by attaching a portable mixer to the handle. To receive a

Lehman's catalog, contact Lehman's, 1 Lehman Circle, P.O. Box 41, Kidron, OH 44636; (330) 857-1111; fax: (330) 857-5785; e-mail: info@lehmans.com.

Peas Porridge in the Pot

Q: *I love to use whole dried green peas in my pea soup, but I never see any information in seed catalogs on what pea varieties would be best to use dried in this manner. Will any variety work just as well as the next?*

A: No. Most of the green pea varieties listed in seed catalogs have a high sugar content because most people will be eating them fresh. These are *not* the types to use for drying, says Will Bonsall, pea curator for the Seed Savers Exchange. The types that are best to use for soup are starchy peas that will cook down to a creamy texture.

Starchy peas that are grown for drying on the plant for soup are called "soup peas" or "field peas." (When you buy dried split peas, you're buying whole dried peas that have been split and skinned.) The legumes known as "Southern peas" are something completely different; and the fact that one category of Southern pea is called "field peas" really makes things confusing.

One easy-to-find green field/soup pea is 'Alaska' (which is also often recommended for fresh eating because of its earliness). It's available from several mail-order sources, including Pinetree Garden Seeds in New Gloucester, Maine. William Dam Seeds in Canada offers two other varieties for drying, including 'Blue Pod Capucijners' and 'Raisin Capucijners' (see "Resources" on page 234).

Not many varieties of field peas are available commercially in this country through seed catalogs, explains Bonsall. But luckily for pea lovers, he propagates close to 800 pea varieties, 100 of which are field peas. Bonsall makes them available to garden preservationists through his Scatterseed Project (P. O. Box 1167, Farmington, ME 04938). Scatterseed is a "germ-plasm conservatory," not a seed company; Bonsall's varieties are listed in the Seed Savers Exchange Yearbook.

A final tip: Bonsall says that if you happen to find whole green peas for cooking in a food store, you can probably use them for seed.

PEPPERS
Bitter Bells

Q: *I grow attractive-looking bell peppers, but they taste bitter. I garden in northern San Diego County where late summer temperatures are often around 100°F and it's sunny all day with no clouds or fog. I fertilize with composted horse manure with a little chicken manure mixed in. The hot peppers I grow taste fine.*

A: A couple things could be going wrong, says Tim Hartz, Ph.D., vegetable specialist with the University of California at Davis. If your pepper plants are extra tall and vigorous and their foliage is very deep dark green, they're getting a lot more nitrogen from all that manure than they need, which could cause bitterness. (Or, as Dr. Hartz puts it, "If you beat a plant over the head with nitrogen, it may pick up some off-flavors.") So don't add any more manure—especially that superpotent chicken stuff—or other nitrogen-rich fertilizers (bloodmeal, fish emulsion, cottonseed meal, etc.) to your pepper patch for a while.

Your hot, cloudless summers could be a source of bitterness, too. Dr. Hartz suggests that you erect a simple structure on which you can hang some shade cloth (a light mesh fabric sold at lawn and garden centers) over the pepper bed to decrease sun and heat.

And we hope you're letting your peppers ripen to red or orange or yellow or whatever their final, ripe color is, aren't you? Green peppers are basically bitter because they're not ripe yet; fully colored peppers are supersweet because their sugar content is at its peak.

Pitiful Peppers

Q: *I grow beautiful bell pepper plants, but the peppers themselves are invariably small and usually misshapen—caricatures of what a pepper should look like. My garden is heavily composted and I use no artificial fertilizer. I've rotated the location of my peppers, and I make sure they receive at least 1 inch of water per week. What am I doing wrong?*

A: What you describe could be a pollination problem, says Chuck Voigt, vegetable specialist with the Illinois Cooperative Extension. This can be caused by weather that's too hot, too cold, or too windy at flowering time. When the weather is too cool, bees aren't active; too warm or windy and the fruit's blossoms may not develop properly. Poor pollination can cause the deformed fruits you describe, he says.

The problem may also lie with your choice of pepper variety. If you're growing an extra-early variety, try switching to a main-season variety, or vice versa, to try to get the plants' flowering time in tune with the kind of weather that favors perfect pollination, says Voigt.

Be sure your plants are getting enough sun as well. (Foliage will grow nicely in partial shade, but the fruit will suffer.) And your problem may be caused by an insect; keep a close eye on your peppers this year to see if you observe any pests hanging around during that crucial late-flower-to-little-pepper period.

Thin-Skinned Peppers

Q: *Our pepper plants remain small and the fruit is thin-skinned and tough. How can we get a better crop?*

A: "Peppers are not the easiest crop to grow," says Dale Kammerlohr, Ph.D., senior plant breeder for Petoseed in Felda, Florida, and breeder of 'North Star' bell pepper. "Don't stress them. Be sure the plants get enough water throughout the season." Another common mistake is setting out transplants that are too old and already beginning to blossom. "Older transplants could set fruit too early, before the plant has developed sufficiently," he says. "Transplants should be ready to set out 6 to 8 weeks from sowing seed. Don't overharden them."

Waiting for Red Bells

Q: *None of my green bell peppers turn red. I even grew 'North Star', which is labeled as "quick to turn red," but still I had no success. What can I do to get red peppers?*

A: Patience, patience, and more patience is the solution to your problem. "There are at least 300 to 400 varieties of bell peppers, and 99 percent of them will ripen from green to red if they're left on the plant long enough," says Ben Villalon, Ph.D., the "Dr. Pepper" of Texas A&M. And red peppers are definitely worth the wait. They look fantastic, taste sweeter, and have twice the vitamin C of green ones.

Cool weather can delay ripening, but that may not be the case where you live. Next time, be sure you start seedlings early enough and get them out into your garden as soon as you can. The number of days listed in the catalog is usually days from transplanting time to harvesting of the first mature green pepper. You have to wait a few more weeks beyond that for red ripe bells. Even 'North Star' pepper, touted as one of the earliest to turn red, needs about 3 weeks to ripen to red from the green stage.

Rose Marie Nichols McGee of Nichols Garden Nursery (purveyors of 'North Star') says you may want to designate a few of your pepper plants as "red pepper" plants. Mark them with a stick if you need to. Don't harvest any green peppers from these plants—by not picking them, you force the plants to push the ripening process along.

Turn Up the Hot Pepper Heat

Q: *Two years ago, I grew cayenne peppers in a spot that was not particularly fertile and that didn't get a lot of water either. I didn't get a lot of peppers and the ones I got were pretty scrawny, but they made a very hot sauce. Last summer, I moved my pepper bed to a more fertile patch and provided more water. I got a bumper crop of cayennes that I stored in the freezer until I had enough to make a really large batch of sauce using the same recipe, but cooked longer. This sauce was nowhere near as hot as the previous year's. Was it the stress?*

A: Too little food and not enough water made your peppers hotter; stress makes hot pepper plants go into overtime on their heat production. "Treat your hot pepper plants miserably and the peppers you harvest will get hotter and hotter and hotter," explains Kat Hardy from the offices of *Chile Pepper* magazine, the periodical for chile heads (1701 River Run, Suite 702, Fort Worth, TX 76107; 888-774-2946) "We get our hottest chiles when the weather is very strange—especially when hot, dry spells alternate with wet ones," she adds.

Freezing or cooking doesn't affect the heat of hot peppers, say the experts at *Chile Pepper*. "The only way to lessen the heat of a hot pepper in the kitchen is to trim out the white placenta that holds the seeds, which is where the hot stuff concentrates," explains Hardy.

POTATOES
Dud Spuds

Q: *I've been growing potatoes for 50 years and still don't know how to beat scab. I heard that sweet (alkaline) soil promotes scab so I put pine needle mulch on the potato patch to promote acidity. But all my potatoes got scab anyway—what can I do to grow smooth-skinned potatoes?*

A: Experts do say that a soil pH at or slightly below 5.5 is best for potato growing—but alkaline soil (a pH above 7.0) is just one of the possible causes of scab (rough, dark patches on potato skin caused by soil-dwelling bacteria that thrive in even mildly alkaline soils). Here's a complete plan to ban these bacteria from your potato beds:

• Have your soil tested to find out just what imbalances exist, then fix them, according to the numbers. Excess alkalinity can be caused by too much calcium, often the result of over-liming the soil. "Too much magnesium or too much potassium may also create a high pH," says Larry Ringer, owner of Ohio Earth Food, a distributor of organic fertilizers. Ringer feels that scab is usually caused by improper fertilization, especially too much nitrogen.

- Plant clean seed potatoes. "Be scrupulous in inspecting your seed potatoes. Don't plant anything that looks like it might be even a little scabby," says Dave Lambert, plant pathologist at the University of Maine (a state that knows its potatoes).

- Plant varieties that resist scab, like these, identified in *Potato Health Management*, edited by Randall C. Rowe (APS Press, 1993): 'Atlantic', 'Belrus', 'Conestoga', 'Crystal', 'Islander', 'Kennebec', 'Larouge', 'Monona', 'Norchip', 'Norgold Russet', 'Norland', 'Onaway', 'Ontario', 'Pungo', 'Rideau', 'Russet Burbank', 'Sebago', 'Superior', and 'Viking'. But don't plant these scab-susceptible varieties: 'Centennial Russet', 'Chippewa', 'Denali', 'Elba', 'Hampton', 'Irish Cobbler', 'Jemseg', 'Kanona', 'Katahdin', 'Red Pontiac', 'Rosa', 'Shepody', 'Steuben', 'White Rose', and 'Yukon Gold.'

- Rotate your crops religiously—don't plant potatoes or other susceptible vegetables like carrots, beets, spinach, turnips, and radishes in the same spot more than once every 4 years.

- Keep the soil of your potato patch at least slightly moist all the time to limit the severity of scab.

- Don't fertilize your potatoes with unfinished compost or raw manure—you will just be giving the scab bacteria something to feed on.

- Grow cover crops but use grains such as rye, millet, or oats instead of legumes such as clover.

CHECK IT OUT!

If you want your potatoes to last longer in storage, try putting some sage, rosemary, and lavender in with them, say researchers in Greece. They found that the essential oils in those herbs suppressed sprouting and inhibited the bacteria that cause potatoes to rot in storage.

Green Potato Truths

Q: *I read somewhere that solanine, the toxic substance associated with green potatoes, breaks down in cooking, making the green parts of the cooked potatoes safe to eat. Is this true? And does all of the potato become toxic when there's a little green showing on the outside—or can you peel away the green parts and safely use the rest? Does solanine also form in potato relatives—like tomatoes and peppers?*

A: Solanine used to be the name that referred to a naturally occurring substance found in the "poisonous" parts of the potato plant, the portions that aren't safe to eat—namely the berries (those little green cherry-tomato-like "fruits" that sometimes appear at the top of potato plants), the leaves, and the sprouts that grow from potato "eyes." But researchers have since discovered that solanine is actually a number of different compounds—which are now known collectively as "glycoalkaloids."

Eating too much of these glycoalkaloids can make you sick (which is why we don't eat other parts of potato plants—just their tubers). Unfortunately, that distinctive green color is not a sure sign of the presence of these compounds, which form when potatoes are stressed—before or after harvest—by exposure to light, cold, drought, cutting, or bruising. The green color is simply a sign that the tubers in question have been exposed to light and have therefore begun to manufacture chlorophyll and turn green.

Although chlorophyll in itself is not toxic, its presence indicates that the potato may also contain high levels of glycoalkaloids due to the exposure to light that made it turn green. "Sometimes green potatoes aren't high in glycoalkaloids, but there's no way to tell just by looking at them," explains Rod Bushway, Ph.D., a professor of food science at the University of Maine.

To further complicate things, some varieties of potato are more susceptible to greening and glycoalkaloid formation than others, notes Mendel Friedman, Ph.D., a scientist with the USDA in Albany, California, whose comprehensive article on glycoalkaloids was published in the journal *Critical Reviews in Plant Sciences* (vol. 16, no.1, 1997).

But contrary to what you've read, "glycoalkaloids are not destroyed during cooking," says Dr. Bushway. In fact, some forms of cooking—baking or frying—may actually concentrate the glycoalkaloids by reducing the water content of the potato.

Al Bushway, Ph.D., also a professor of food science at the University of Maine (and brother of the other Dr. Bushway), reports that he participated in a study in 1984 "in which several people ate cooked potatoes that we knew contained high levels of glycoalkaloids, and all came down with typical symptoms of food poisoning." His brother Rod, one of the first scientists to analyze potatoes chemically, adds that "you probably could cut away all of the green and be all right eating what's left" but adds that some glycoalkaloids could remain.

The bottom line? None of the experts we spoke with recommends eating green potatoes. Dr. Friedman adds the caution that pregnant women—or those who might soon become pregnant—should avoid green potatoes completely, as should anyone with any kind of existing medical problem.

In the garden, you can minimize the chance of harvesting glycoalkaloid-rich spuds by growing your potatoes as stress-free as possible: Give them a rich, balanced soil, a nice thick sunlight-proof mulch, and plenty of water; harvest them on time; handle them gently; and store them in a humid, dark, cool (not freezing) place. And if a potato—green or not—tastes bitter, don't eat it. "Glycoalkaloids don't taste very good," says Dr. Al Bushway, who knows.

And finally, the leaves of potato relatives such as peppers and tomatoes do contain glycoalkaloids. They're different than the ones in potatoes, but their effect can be the same—too much can make you sick. Again, it's good practice to grow these plants as stress-free as possible— and don't eat too many fried green tomatoes either. "Green tomatoes contain a glycoalkaloid called tomatine, which disappears as the tomato ripens," says Dr. Rod Bushway.

Pinch Your Potatoes

Q: *I've heard several theories about getting the best potato crop. Longtime gardeners tell me to pinch the flowers off the plant to encourage growth back to the root. The other theory involves how much water potato plants need: Some say they like it wet, others say they like it dry. I'm confused.*

A: The flower theory: Potato flowers look nice, but they take away energy that could be used for tuber production, says Robert Leiby, cooperative extension agent for Lehigh County in Pennsylvania. Pinching the flower buds before they open will free up more energy for tuber production. "It's not practical on a commercial scale, but if you have the time to do it, go ahead." he says.

The water theory: Francis Pollock, a potato grower in Monroe County, Pennsylvania, says that potatoes need good amounts of water, but only at specific times. Water is especially important when the tubers are beginning to set shortly after the plant flowers. When the tubers are bulking up, they need even, moderate amounts of water. Too much moisture at irregular intervals can result in hollow hearts. Potatoes also don't do well in soggy, poorly drained soils.

Potato Cherries? Berries? What Are These Things?

Q: *Clusters of strange whatchamacallits grew from the top of my potato plants this year. They look like tiny tomatoes, but I'm sure they're not. What are these? Do potatoes have seedpods? Or should I call them pomatoes?*

A: Potato fruit (or seed balls) they are, say our potato experts. They look like tomatoes because the two plants are so closely related and produce fruit in the same way. (Unlike tomato fruit, potato fruit is inedible.) They were a surprise to you because not all potato varieties produce these seedpods, and even the ones that do don't do it every year. Conditions have to be just right, says Ken Steffen, Ph.D., assistant professor of vegetable crops at Penn State University.

Under optimal conditions, potato pollen landing on the female flower part will germinate and grow into the seed embryo in the ovary located in the base of the flower. When the embryo is fertilized in this way, a hormone causes the ovary to swell and grow.

Whether the seed contained in these pods is viable depends on how the four sets of chromosomes inside match up. Even if the seed is viable, chances are slim that it will grow into a potato that's as good as the one from which it's sprung. That's why most potatoes are propagated from tubers, says Dr. Steffen.

Tough Potatoes

Q: *Last year I planted red potatoes on February 14. When I dug them up on June 1, they were a beautiful color and a nice size but so hard that they were not fit*

to eat. My garden, which usually grows good potatoes, has sandy soil. I used packaged fertilizer and some barnyard manure and side-dressed with bonemeal. What am I doing wrong?

A: "Your problem may be caused by a nutrient imbalance related to the calcium/magnesium ratio in the soil," suggests Ed Plissey, extension potato specialist at the University of Maine. Such imbalances can cause calcium and magnesium to move to a potato's cell walls and make those walls very firm. In addition, Plissey adds that "some red-skinned potato varieties already have very low 'solids' compared to the other types of potatoes, and that makes them more susceptible to this kind of malady."

Plissey says that the types of fertilizers you're using appear to be fine, but that the proportions "could be out of whack." He recommends you have your soil tested; the results will reveal whether you need to add some lime or sul-po-mag to balance the nutrients. Request soil test instructions from your local cooperative extension office. (You'll find their number listed under the county offices in your phone directory.)

RADISHES
Skinny Radishes

Q: *The radishes I've planted the last 3 years have refused to "ball up" although their leaves always looked lush and bug-free. Last year, I planted kohlrabi and it did the same thing. The stems make a 90-degree turn at the ground, go about 1½ to 2 inches on the ground, and then make another 90-degree turn into the ground. I thin them according to the packet. What am I doing wrong?*

A: Jim Stephens, extension vegetable specialist at the University of Florida, suggests two possibilities: 1) Did you over-fertilize your plants? "Excessive nitrogen in the soil can cause lots of leaf growth but very thin, elongated roots," explains Stephens, who wrote his master's thesis on the effects of fertilizer and moisture on the growth of radishes. 2) Did you plant these cool-weather-loving crops late in spring? "If temperatures get too high, the roots won't enlarge," he says. You should sow radishes as soon as you can work the ground in spring; and try seeding your kohlrabi in midsummer for a fall crop.

Also, check your radish variety—some new hybrids have been bred to be grown in greenhouses and might not bulb up otherwise. And some radishes are adapted to grow best only in certain climates during certain times of the year. "In Florida, we grow 'Cherry Belle' in the fall and through the winter, but in the spring it becomes very spindly and pencil-shaped, so we switch to other varieties," says Stephens. So try growing a variety that's specifically recommended for spring planting in your region. Your county cooperative extension office should be able to offer some suggestions.

Raising Radish Seeds

Q: *I love sprouted radish seeds and would like to grow some radishes for their seeds this summer. Any recommendations?*

A: You can order a quarter pound of radish seeds from Johnny's Selected Seeds in Albion, Maine (make sure you buy untreated seeds). You can plant as many of the seeds as you want and use the rest to make your own sprouts until your crop matures. To harvest your radish seeds, cut the

Here's another way to enjoy the zinginess of radishes: Grow 'Rat's Tail' (Raphanus sativus var. caudatus), a unique heirloom radish that has edible foot-long seedpods! 'Rat's Tail' grows 4 to 5 feet tall and produces a plethora of pods in 50 days, explains Dick Meiners of Pinetree Gardens in New Gloucester, Maine. Enjoy the spicy pods raw in salads, or use them to add zip to your stir-fries.

seed stalks after they're dry, and rub or gently pound the pods to release the seeds.

You might also want to check out edible-pod radishes. 'Rat's Tail' is an heirloom radish with pungent 8- to 16-inch-long pods that you can eat raw, pickled, or cooked. It's offered by J. L. Hudson, Seedsman. The 'Madras' radish produces large quantities of tender, slightly sweet 2- to 3-inch seedpods, which you can eat whole before they mature and turn hard. It's available from Bountiful Gardens. (See "Resources" on page 234 for addresses.)

RHUBARB

Harvesting Rhubarb

Q: *I would like some information on when and how to pick rhubarb. I've heard that you should pick only during certain months. Is that true? I've always pulled the stalks out from the root.*

A: Rhubarb stalks are at their best when they are large and juicy. Later in the season, they turn dry and taste "punky," says Bernard Zandstra, Ph.D., vegetable specialist at Michigan State University. If you missed your picking "window," cut the plant down to the ground, and the stalks will regrow in time to give you a second, tender harvest in late summer or fall, says Dr. Zandstra. Pulling out the stalks is a good way to harvest but so is cutting the stalks at ground level, he adds.

Toxic Leaves?

Q: *I've read that rhubarb leaves are toxic. Is it safe to put them into my compost pile?*

A: Yes. Although it's not safe to eat rhubarb leaves, compost that has been made with some rhubarb leaves will not hurt your soil or plants. Some gardeners use large flat rhubarb leaves as mulch around transplants temporarily to prevent weed seeds from sprouting.

SWEET POTATOES
Bitter Sweets

Q: *We have a bad problem with our sweet potatoes. They have black spots on the outside and they are bitter. Is the problem in the soil or on the plants I buy? I use different plots of land to grow them each season, but this seems to make no difference. Someone told me to dip the plants in a solution. Can you tell me what to use?*

A: Sounds like black rot, says Barbara Pleasant, a garden writer from way down in sweet potato heaven (a.k.a. Alabama). Black rot is a fungal disease that may develop in the garden or in storage. It can persist for 2 or 3 years in the soil, but it can also be spread by soil-dwelling insects that feed on sweet potatoes and wild morning glory (so keep your sweet-potato patch free of these weeds).

The first thing you should do is start with disease-free plants. Look for "certified" sweet potato slips, meaning that they're certified disease-free. If you grow your own slips, cut them at least ½ inch away from the spot where they join the mother tuber.

Be sure to follow a strict 3-year rotation, adds Anthony Keinath, Ph.D., assistant professor of plant pathology at Clemson University in South Carolina. That is, wait a full 3 years before planting sweet potatoes in the same place again. And yes, for extra insurance, there is a "solution" solution as well: Soak your sweet potato slips in a solution of 3 ounces of borax powder to 1 gallon of water for 10 minutes right before you plant them.

Sometimes black rot disease appears after the sweet potatoes are in storage. Proper curing can help to prevent this. Dry your sweet potatoes in a warm place that's about 85°F for a good week, then store them in a dry, airy place at about 60°F. Don't wash the potatoes before storage; it can spread the disease.

Bad Variety Choice

Q: *Last year, I grew 'Georgia Jet' sweet potatoes, but unfortunately they weren't sweet at all. What went wrong with them?*

A: Those unsweet potatoes sound like a bad variety choice. 'Georgia Jet' is a potato known for its ability to stay moist when you cook it and not for its sweetness, explains Mel Henninger, Ph.D., vegetable crops extension specialist at Rutgers University in New Jersey. If it's sweetness you want, try 'Ivis White Cream', a white-skinned, white-fleshed heirloom sold by the Sand Hill Preservation Center.

Oh, and for maximum sweetness with any variety, you have to "cure" your sweet potatoes. "When you first dig them up, they'll taste more starchy and less sweet than they will after you cure them," says Dr. Henninger. To cure sweet potatoes, place them in a warm (85° to 90°F), humid spot for 1 week. (Putting them in a plastic bag next to your basement heater should work. Just be sure to leave the top of the bag open so that moisture can escape.) Curing changes a lot of the potato's starches to sugars, making the flesh sweeter. Curing also heals injuries to the skin, allowing your harvest to last longer in storage, adds Dr. Henninger.

One Sick Tomato

Q: *Last year we raised our tomatoes from seed and all were fine except one 'Celebrity' plant. Its leaves turned up and in, and the plant eventually became infested with whitefly and scale. If this happens again, what should we do?*

A: Upward curling of leaves on tomatoes can signify the presence of a virus, or it can be a sign of nutritional or insect problems, says Jane E. Polston, Ph.D., plant virologist and associate professor at the University of Florida. Because just one plant was affected rather than most of them, a virus or insect is most likely to blame. If the symptoms are severe, remove the entire plant to keep the disease or insect from spreading.

Also, if you handle tobacco products, you can avoid introducing or spreading the tobacco mosaic virus to your tomatoes by thoroughly washing your hands before touching your tomato plants. And to minimize the risk of spreading seedborne viruses, "save seed only from really healthy-looking plants," suggests Dr. Polston.

Upward curling on leaves could also indicate a nutrient imbalance. If the symptoms show up in more than one plant, consider having your soil tested.

Tasteless Tomatoes

Q: *We planted 'Century' and 'Early Girl' tomatoes last year and had some problems. They were big, red, and pretty on the outside, but inside there was a big, hard, white core and a white, lacy layer under the skin, and they had no flavor. Our county agent said other people*

A: A combination of radical swings in soil moisture and attacks by stinkbugs are the most likely causes of your hard-core problem, says Chuck Marr, Ph.D., extension vegetable specialist at Kansas State University.

Those big white cores and/or white, lacy layers can be caused by irregular watering—the same conditions that can cause blossom-end rot, says Dr. Marr. (Blossom-end rot usually looks like a big black spot on the portion of the tomato farthest away from the stem.)

Dr. Marr says that mulching your tomato plants well is the best way to keep soil moisture nice and even. Drip irrigation helps a lot, too. But however you water, keep it constant, avoiding extremes of wet and dry.

And don't forget those stinkbugs: When the insects puncture the skin of a tomato to feed, they cause a discoloration on top and a whitish, corky layer in the tissue below the skin. "If the feeding is excessive, the spots sort of run together," says Dr. Marr.

Keep stinkbugs off your tomatoes with a floating row cover, and don't plant next to a wild area where stinkbugs can build up a strong population and then move into the garden. Plant herbs like dill and fennel and allow them to flower; those flowers will attract stinkbug predators with their pollen and nectar.

Weird Tomatoes

Q: *My parents' tomato plants developed knobby stems soon after they were transplanted into the garden. The plants were stunted and production was very limited, although the plants seemed to revive* *a bit at the end of the season. What is the problem, and how can we keep it from occurring next year?*

A: The deformation you describe is probably a condition known as "adventitious roots," says Charles McClurg, Ph.D., extension vegetable specialist at the University of Maryland. Adventitious roots are roots that grow somewhere other than where they're supposed to (such as the outer surface of the stem), and rest assured, your plants aren't the only ones to have suffered this seemingly odd affliction. "A woman once drove for an hour in Beltway rush-hour traffic with a similar tomato plant that she wanted me to see," says Dr. McClurg.

Adventitious roots frequently form on plants that have lots of lush leaves above and moist ground below, explains Dr. McClurg. But sometimes the cause is more sinister: "Some herbicides such as 2,4-D [often used by homeowners and lawn-care companies to kill dandelions] can drift onto tomato plants and cause strange-looking stems, too," he adds.

To prevent this condition, give your tomato plants lots of room so the leaves can dry between rains, don't overwater, and, of course, don't use herbicides.

Battle Plan for Early Blight

Q: *I'm having trouble growing tomatoes. At first, the plants grow beautifully and have gorgeous fruit, but then brown spots start appearing on the leaves at the bottom of the plants and work their way up, eventually killing the plant. I think the problem is early blight. Can you tell me how to get rid of it?*

A: Your problem does sound like early blight, but it could also be septoria leaf spot. With early blight, the brown spots have dark concentric rings, like a target; with septoria, the

Although homemade soap sprays made from dishwashing detergent may be inexpensive and convenient for controlling pests like aphids and whiteflies, you'll get better results from commercial insecticidal soap products (such as Concern's or Safer's). Several reports indicate the homemade sprays are slightly toxic to many plants. In contrast, commercial insecticidal soap products are specifically formulated for insect control and go easier on the treated plants.

spots are tan or gray with dark brown margins and tiny black dots in the center. Both of these diseases start on the lower leaves of a plant and work their way up, both are caused by a fungus, and both develop in warm, moist conditions.

And the severity of both can be reduced with similar methods. Here are some of the recommendations from Ruth V. Hazzard and Robert L. Wick of the University of Massachusetts Extension and Agroecology Program, which appeared in a recent issue of *The Natural Farmer*, a great newspaper for growers published by the Northeast Organic Farming Association. (We've adapted the recommendations for gardeners.)

- Wait at least 3 years before planting tomatoes (or potatoes or eggplants, which are also susceptible to these diseases) in the same spot, just in case some of the disease survives from year to year. And don't plant susceptible crops (tomatoes, potatoes, and eggplants) next to each other in the garden. "Disease can spread from one vegetable to another," writes Hazzard.

- Have your soil tested and make any necessary adjustments to ensure that your tomatoes have proper nutrition. Add organic matter yearly to ensure a steady supply of nitrogen and to feed beneficial soil organisms.

- Select tomato varieties that are disease-tolerant and use high-quality, disease-free seed. 'Mountain Supreme' from Dr. Randy Gardner's breeding program at North Carolina State University has good early blight resistance. Unfortunately, no tomatoes are currently available that are resistant to septoria leaf spot, says Jim Waltrip of Petoseed in Felda, Florida, but he adds that they're working hard on it. (You can get 'Mountain Supreme' from Tomato Growers Supply; see "Resources" on page 234.)

- Keep your transplants as healthy as possible; reduce early-season stress from cold or wind with row covers and windbreaks. "Do anything you can to prevent plant stress," writes Hazzard.

- Help the leaves of your plants dry off quickly after rains by planting them where they'll get lots of morning sun, staking or caging the plants, and spacing them far enough apart so air can circulate around them. "If leaves are dry, the disease spores can't germinate and penetrate the leaf," explains Hazzard.
- Don't work in the garden when leaves are wet. You could spread disease spores and make an infection worse.

Tied into Late Blight?

Q: *My tomato plants had late blight last year. The plants were tied to stakes with jute string, and I'd like to reuse the string but am concerned about spreading the blight onto this year's plants. Could the string harbor the disease?*

A: Late blight is a fungal disease spread by wind-blown spores of *Phytophthora infestans*. These spores are everywhere, and yes, they're probably on your string right now. But the critical factor that will determine whether your tomatoes come down with late blight this year is not the presence of the spores but the weather, says Tim Hartz, Ph.D., extension vegetable specialist with the University of California at Davis.

"Dry weather keeps the fungus from growing, and a long period of rain, fog, or dew keeps tomato leaves wet and encourages the development of the disease," explains Dr. Hartz. "Personally, I wouldn't worry about using the string over again. The string itself is not going to support the growth of the fungus. If you do see late blight again, it's probably not from the twine."

The best way to prevent a reoccurrence of late blight is to compost or bury last year's infected plants. The late blight fungus usually survives the winter in plant debris, especially potato tubers, but it won't survive in or on the ground, says our East Coast plant disease expert, Robert L. Wick, Ph.D., a plant pathologist with the University of Massachusetts. For extra insurance against late blight, you could "boil the twine in water to kill any disease organisms that might survive there," he adds.

Taking the Droop out of Tomatoes

Q: *How can I stop my tomato plants from wilting after they reach maturity?*

A: Your problem is probably southern sclerotium wilt, or more commonly southern blight (*Sclerotium rolfsii*). It's a fungus that infects more than 200 different plants, including most vegetables. There's not a lot you can do to remedy this once the tomatoes are wilting, but next year be sure you plant the tomatoes in a different spot, and try solarizing the soil. When your tomatoes are in their new spot, keep organic matter away from their stems, and keep the soil around those stems dry.

Southern blight is a problem across most of the South because the soilborne fungus that causes southern blight thrives on moisture and high temperatures. "Southern blight is a warm-season disease," says Craig Andersen, Ph.D., vegetable specialist at the University of Arkansas. "The fungus is dormant when the soil temperature is below 68°F."

As soon as the soil warms, the fungus grows on organic matter near the stem. The first symptom of infection is a dark brown lesion just below the soil surface on the succulent stem. Usually, though, the first symptom you notice is progressive yellowing or wilting of foliage, beginning with the lowest leaves. By then, the disease has already begun to eat away at the outer part of the stem and will eventually girdle the plant and kill it. Remove any wilting plants as soon as you find them, and burn them. "Don't compost the plants," Dr. Andersen says. "This fungus is tough. It can survive composting."

Plant tomatoes in a fresh site every year, and if possible leave the infected site fallow for at least 3 years. If you can't do that, plant cool-season crops there instead—they'll be just about finished by the time the soil warms enough to promote southern blight. Take the plot out of production in July and August, the hottest months, and solarize it. "Solarizing seems to help combat southern blight," Dr. Andersen says. In subsequent seasons, grow a partly resistant crop such as sweet corn to help reduce the amount of the disease in that patch.

"The fungus is opportunistic and needs decaying organic matter to feed on," Dr. Andersen explains. To help prevent the fungus at your new site, don't use any organic mulch near the plant—put sand or pebbles around it for mulch instead. And clean up any leaves that fall off—they can provide food to fuel the fungus.

Crew-Cut Tomatoes

Q: *My tomatoes get 8 feet tall by the end of the growing season. To keep them manageable, I'd like to cut them off when they get to be 6 feet tall. Would this hurt the plants or my crop?*

A: Clip away. "It doesn't hurt to cut the tops off tomato plants if they get too tall," assures Doug Sanders, Ph.D., extension specialist and professor at North Carolina State University. In fact, it could even improve your crop. "The plant will produce more branches and flowers below the cut," he explains, "and you'll probably get larger fruits overall as well."

Sad Seedlings

Q: *Two weeks after emerging, my tomato seedlings turn purple, become sickly, and often die. If they live, the plants will be small. I grow them under fluorescent lights and have a water softener. Could this be a problem? The rest of my plants always do well.*

A: Although long-distance diagnosis of such a problem is tricky at best, your plants may have a phosphorus deficiency, suggests our seed-starting expert, Nancy Bubel. The purple color and the stunting are both classic symptoms of such a food shortage.

What kind of soil (or soilless) medium are you using to start your seeds? One part finished compost and one part vermiculite is the light, fertile combination recommended by Bubel in her book, *The New Seed-Starters Handbook* (Rodale, 1988). Then, every 10 days to 2 weeks, after the true leaves emerge, you should give your seedlings a balanced feeding by watering with a half-strength solution of fish emulsion. And yes—if your water softener is the type that uses salt, don't use this treated water on your plants—it may contain a lot of sodium.

Tomato Blossom Drop

Q: *A friend gave me some tomato seeds from Italy that had been passed down to him by his grandfather, and his before him, and so on. Each time I've planted them, the plants get real big with lots of flowers, but the flowers just fall off before turning to tomatoes. Why? Can you give me tips to ensure a good harvest?*

A: Sounds as if those tomato seeds come from plants that have been growing in the same little corner of Italy for a long time, and "the tomato has probably become very adapted to the climate in that specific region," says Craig LeHoullier, an heirloom tomato grower from North Carolina. It's likely that the conditions where you live aren't similar to the original growing conditions, and therefore aren't the type that this particular tomato needs to properly set fruit. "Every tomato has its own temperature range in which pollination occurs," he explains, "and the flowers will fall off if temperatures are outside of that range."

LeHoullier's advice is to try planting your tomato seeds earlier or later—when your temps may be more conducive to fruit set for this variety. And when the flowers open, gently tap them to help move their pollen from the stamens to the pistils, so that fertilization can occur more easily.

If that still doesn't work, consider asking your friend to share some seeds with a preservation society such as the Seed Savers Exchange, so that people in other climates could try growing them and saving their seeds.

Thick-Skinned Tomatoes

Q: *I've noticed that I've been getting very thick skins on my tomatoes for the past two seasons. I usually grow several varieties including 'Better Boy' and 'Early Girl.' What's causing the problem with their skins?*

A: "Thick tomato skins are caused by lack of water and real hot temperatures," explains Sharon Kaszan, supervisor of Burpee's trial gardens. "The plant makes the skins thick to protect the flesh inside. And we've had some really hot, dry summers recently," she adds.

The solution? "If we have another hot summer, give each plant at least 1 gallon of water every 2 or 3 days to keep it growing consistently and evenly, and mulch the plants to

CHECK IT OUT!

Here's one way to help make your tomato seedlings grow strong and stocky, so they'll be able withstand the harsh spring winds after you plant them outside: Tickle them every day! Research has shown that brushing the tops of the plants lightly for 1½ minutes twice a day keeps the plants short while the stems grow thicker. You can follow noted gardener and author Eliot Coleman's example and brush your seedlings with an old piece of row cover tied to a stick.

keep the soil and roots cool," she suggests. Kaszan adds that she feels that cherry tomatoes with tough skins are the worst tomatoes to try to bite into.

Tiny Tomatoes

Q: *I grow vegetables in 2-foot planters. I feed the tomatoes with liquid tomato food every weekend, and they get full sun all afternoon. The first 2 years I had problems with blossom-end rot. Now the tomatoes produce a lot of fruit, but all of it is small. I expected medium-size slicing tomatoes, but none grew larger than a golf ball. What am I doing wrong?*

A: Sounds like you're trying to grow tomatoes in an oven. Full afternoon sun will absolutely bake container plants sitting on a sizzling deck or patio, "which can have a negative effect on fruit size," says Charlie O'Dell, extension horticulturist at Virginia Polytechnic Institute. And your "small fruit and history of blossom-end rot indicate that you are watering the plants unevenly," adds Herman Hohlt, Ph.D., extension vegetable specialist at the Eastern Shore Agricultural Research and Extension Center in Painter, Virginia. He suggests that you pay close attention to the moistness of your growing medium and "aim for constant, even moisture."

"By the time they get to be 3 or 4 feet high, container-grown tomatoes can need water two or three times a day. If you can't tend these pots daily, some kind of a watering system would be in order," says Dr. Hohlt, who suggests a simple "reservoir and wick system," in which the reservoir is a pot of water and the wick is in the water with the other end touching the soil in the container.

What's more, the fertilizer you've been using is not organic; it's a harsh chemical salt and it sounds like you've been using too much of it (of course, we think a molecule of this stuff is too much, but you've probably been using too much even for a chemical gardener). "If the concentration of fertilizer is as high as it sounds, you might be developing a salt problem in your pots," agrees Dr. Hohlt.

So, to begin with, empty your containers and start fresh this year with new soil, amended with nice, nutritious, gentle, organic compost. Set up your watering system and, if your containers are black or dark-colored, paint them with white latex paint so they'll reflect some of that hot direct sunlight instead of absorbing it all. And If you just have to feed your plants regularly, do so with a weak fish emulsion or liquid seaweed solution.

Tomato Troubles

Q: *Extension agents at the University of Connecticut have identified fusarium and verticillium fungi in my soil. They sent me a list of resistant tomato varieties, but I have been using my own heritage seeds for the past 15 to 20 years and want to continue. Each spring I start about 100 plants; the ones I give away do beautifully, but mine all die. I hope someone can give me some information on how to cure my garden, which is only 24 × 30 feet.*

A: Once these tomato disease pathogens are in your soil, getting rid of them takes a long time. Is there a spot in your garden where tomatoes haven't grown for at least 4 years? If there is, try planting one of your heirlooms there this year.

Even if a tomato plant does become infected, you may be able to keep it growing and fruiting, says Sharon Douglas, Ph.D., plant pathologist at the University of Connecticut Agricultural Experiment Station. Give it fertile soil, good drainage, and uniform water. "Often a mulch will help," Dr. Douglas adds. At the end of the season, pull up any infected plants quickly to avoid overwintering disease spores, and don't save seed from an infected plant.

But if your garden soil is as thoroughly and heavily infested as it sounds, your other option—one that works extremely well, by the way—is to grow your tomatoes in large containers filled with new, uncontaminated soil. (You can even place the containers themselves on top of the contaminated soil if that's your only sunny spot.)

Tough Tomatoes

Q: *For the past few years, my tomatoes have had hard green shoulders and generally do not ripen to the stem. My garden has early blight, so I grow resistant varieties such as 'Celebrity', 'Heatwave', and 'Quick Pic.' Last year, the hot humid weather caused some early blight, and again the tomatoes had hard green tops. Are the two related and what can I do?*

A: Some tomato varieties tend to have hard green shoulders more than others; and this problem will occur when the fruits of any variety are exposed to the sun. Because early blight causes plants to drop leaves, your green tops were probably related to the lack of sun protection caused by the blight. Here's what you can do:

Steve Garrison, Ph.D., vegetable specialist with the Rutgers Cooperative Extension in Bridgeton, New Jersey, says that staking is essential, so if you're not already staking your tomatoes, start doing so—arranging the vines so that the leaves shade as much fruit as possible. If you already stake your vines, try draping your plants with shade cloth to protect the exposed fruits from the sun if blight strikes again.

Another possibility: Sometimes ripening problems are caused by a mineral imbalance, particularly a lack of potassium in combination with an excess of nitrogen, explains

Dr. Garrison. So if you haven't had your soil tested lately, do so. If potassium levels are low, compost and an occasional application of granite meal or greensand should do the trick.

Oh, and next year try growing 'Mountain Supreme' tomatoes. This variety from Randy Gardener, Ph.D., tomato breeder at North Carolina State University, is extremely resistant to early blight, says Dr. Garrison. (You can order seeds from Tomato Growers Supply; see "Resources" on page 234.)

Nonstop Sauce Tomatoes

Q: *Is there such a thing as an indeterminate paste tomato? If so, where can I get some seeds?*

A: Indeterminate (tomatoes whose vines continue to grow and produce as long as the season permits) paste tomatoes are few and far between——probably because most people (and companies) who process tomatoes like to harvest big batches of fruits all at once (which is how determinate vines produce their crop).

Luckily, Tomato Growers Supply (TGS) offers an unusually large selection of nonstop pasters, including 'Palestinian', 'Polish Giant Paste' and 'Amish Paste'. All three varieties produce large (½ pound and up), red, oblong tomatoes, with the first ripe ones arriving about 85 days after transplanting. Other indeterminate pasters offered by TGS include: 'San Marzano' (fruits are slightly smaller and earlier—80 days); 'Super Marzano' (a hybrid version whose 5-inch fruits begin to ripen in a super-early 70 days); 'Sausage' (6-inch-long fruits in 78 days); and 'Super Italian Paste' (6-inch-long fruits in 73 days).

Shepherd's Garden Seeds carries an indeterminate paste tomato as well: 'San Remo', whose vigorous vines bear clusters of fat, elongated fruits, starting 76 days after transplanting. And 'Opalka', a banana-pepper–shaped paster from Poland, is available from Seed Savers Exchange's Heirloom Seeds and Gifts catalog. (See "Resources" on page 234 for addresses.)

ZUCCHINI

Mutant Zukes

Q: *I had a bountiful, beautiful garden last year, except for the mutated zucchini. The blossom end didn't seal itself up. I used seeds left over from the previous year, and I had no problems like this then. Can you explain?*

A: Your zucchini apparently experienced a hormonal imbalance that may have been due to weather stress. "Nobody knows exactly why it happens," says Colen Wyatt, Ph.D., a vegetable breeder for Seminis Vegetable Seeds in Woodland, California, but sometimes deformities like these are related to cool spring temperatures or lack of sunlight, he explains.

Luckily, your squash aberration is probably a onetime occurrence, says Dr. Wyatt. But to ensure that your plants form perfect squash in the future, grow them in rich, fertile soil and give them lots of water. Try growing early hybrid varieties, which are generally more adaptable to spring conditions, he suggests.

Shriveled Squash

Q: *There's something wrong with my zucchini. The plants and flowers look great and the fruits start out great, but when they get to be 3 or 4 inches long, they just shrivel up. No signs of bugs inside. Any clues?*

A: It sounds like inadequate pollination, says Stephen Buchmann, Ph.D., cofounder of the Forgotten Pollinators Campaign at the Arizona-Sonora Desert Museum in Tucson. Zucchinis frequently shrivel at that size if the female flower only receives a few pollen grains (from a single visit by a bee) instead of the hundreds it needs to set a full-size healthy fruit, he explains.

Zucchini is pollinated by honeybees, bumblebees, and a couple species of wild native bees commonly called squash and gourd bees. Squash bees are immune to the parasitic mites that are reducing honeybee numbers, but there may have been low numbers of these squash pollinators in your area due to a bad winter, bad weather, or pesticide use, says Dr. Buchmann.

To attract more squash and gourd bees this season, try leaving some areas of unmulched soil in and around your garden, suggests Dr. Buchmann, who explains that these bees build their nests in the ground under bare soil. And avoid overwatering, which could flood out their nests.

If your zucchini failure repeats itself this year, try hand-pollinating. John Navazio, Ph.D., a breeder at Alf Christianson Seed Company in Mt. Vernon, Washington, recommends this technique: Break off two or three male flowers (the ones with smooth stems), peel back the petals, and rub the pollen-bearing anthers of each flower into the center of the female flower (the one with a small, immature fruit attached).

CHECK IT OUT!

Zucchini that starts out strong but declines as the season progresses may be suffering from a virus or powdery mildew. So next season, try growing the ultra disease-resistant variety called 'Whitaker'. 'Whitaker' resists powdery mildew and three viruses that are spread by aphids. Seed is available from Territorial Seed Company (see "Resources" on page 234).

Chapter

2

FLOWERS

**Growing beautiful flowers is one
of the most rewarding aspects of
gardening. But what do you do when
you end up with petal-less peonies or
your snapdragons develop rust? You'll
find the answers to those questions in
the pages that follow, along with some
other sound advice for getting the
most out of your flowers.**

BEAUTIFUL BULBS
The Art of Bulb Forcing

Q: *I tried to force some tulip bulbs to bloom indoors but failed. I put 20 bulbs in the refrigerator, left them there for 2 months, then I planted them in a bowl, covered them with plastic wrap, and put them back in the refrigerator for 1 more month. Then I moved the planter to a sunny window. The tulips grew fine for a while but died when they were about 5 inches tall. What did I do wrong?*

A: First, you must plant the bulbs in "the pot in which they are going to bloom," says Art Wolk of Voorhees, New Jersey, bulb-forcing expert and former winner of the Philadelphia Flower Show's grand sweepstakes prize. And "if you put the bulbs in a refrigerator, it is crucial that it doesn't also contain fruit because the ethylene gas that is naturally released by the fruit can kill the flower buds," he adds.

Here's Wolk's easy plan for forcing bulbs: In the fall, plant the bulbs in containers that have holes in the bottom for drainage and that are filled with a very loose and porous, premoistened potting mix. "A good mix is 60 percent sphagnum peat moss, 20 percent perlite, and 20 percent vermiculite," suggests Wolk. "Then put the container outdoors in a hole in the ground. About 18 inches deep should work in colder soil; it can be closer to the surface in milder climates. Cover the pot with soil, then add 1 to 2 feet of organic mulch [chopped leaves, straw, etc.] on top of everything to keep the soil from freezing hard. Put a long stick in the ground next to the pot so you can find it in case it gets covered by snow.

"About 3 months later, remove the mulch, dig down carefully, and remove the pot. Use a hose to clean off the pot and shoots, then bring the pot indoors to a bright sunny room where temperatures will range between 60° and 68°F. Depending on the cultivar of tulip you choose, you'll have blooms in 3 to 6 weeks," he predicts.

If outdoor digging is not your idea of winter fun, and you prefer to start the bulbs in a refrigerator, make *sure* that the fridge contains no fruit; and that the temperature is set between 45° to 50°F—"the best range for rooting," says Wolk. Plant the bulbs in the container, as Wolk has already described; *don't* cover the container with plastic wrap, then set it in the refrigerator for about 3 months. When you take the container out, set it in indirect light for the first 4 days because the first (light-colored) leaves will probably be showing and you don't want to burn them. *Then* move the container into a cool, bright sunny room—and get ready to enjoy the show.

Saving Potted Daffodils

Q: *How should I handle my potted daffodils after they've finished blooming?*

A: If the potted daffodils aren't hardy, Becky Heath of Brent and Becky's Bulbs in Gloucester, Virginia, recommends throwing the bulbs away and starting again next year. "Usually the show is disappointing in the second and third seasons," she says.

You can save hardy varieties, however. As long as the foliage is green, water well and then let dry thoroughly. Keep

CHECK IT OUT!

If you'd like to have some individual blooms to plug into container gardens in the spring, try this easy forcing technique: Fill pots (at least 3 inches wide × 4 inches deep) with potting soil, leaving about 1 inch of space at the top. Place one bulb in each pot, and pack some more soil around the bulb (but don't bury it). Put the pots into a nursery flat, place the flat outside in a shaded area, and cover it with 6 to 8 inches of leaves. Water occasionally, and your bulbs will be ready to plant in about 12 weeks.

the pot in good light. When foliage dies down, put the pot or just the bulbs in a dry location. In November, pot the bulbs and start over again.

For hardy varieties, Heath advises planting them outside, usually in June, because they're heavy feeders and hard to maintain in a pot. Root growth will begin because ground temperature is usually cooler than the air.

Scarce Saffron

Q: *After a sensational first season of growing saffron flowers, I've experienced 2 years of poor blossoming. What's wrong?*

A: "The corms may be too small, says Peter de Jager, owner of Peter de Jager Bulb Company in South Hamilton, Massachusetts, a supplier of saffron corms. "Saffron crocus (*Crocus sativus*) corms less than 8 centimeters (about 3 inches) in circumference won't blossom."

If your plants are closer than 4 inches apart, over-crowding might be limiting bulb size. Divide older corms at least every 3 years—preferably in summer after the foliage has died—but only replant corms that are larger than 8 centimeters around, de Jager says. Smaller saffron corms often take 3 years to blossom.

Plant corms in late summer or early fall (generally August through October) in a hole three times the height of the bulb, with the root sides facing down. Well-drained soil and full sun to light shade are best. Avoid fertilizing when leaves are sprouting. Your saffron should bloom in about 6 weeks.

Although easy to grow and hardy in most parts of the United States, saffron corms benefit from a protective mulch in areas with severe winters.

FIGURING OUT FLOWERS

All-Foliage Begonias

Q: *My 2-year-old angelwing begonia grows beautiful foliage but won't bloom. What am I doing wrong?*

A: Light and pot size affect begonia flowering. "Good light will bring on flowering for most angelwing varieties," says Tovah Martin of Logee's Greenhouses in Danielson, Connecticut, a supplier of rare plants. "A bright east or west window is best."

In addition, begonias are fussy about container size, and too large a pot could inhibit bloom. "Roots should fill the pot, although the plant should not be rootbound. When potting, use a container just one size larger," says Mildred Thompson, author of *Begonias—The Complete Reference Guide* (Times Books, 1981).

Angelwings bloom at various times of the year, depending on the variety. 'Orange Rubra', 'Elaine', and 'Jim Wyrtzen' all are considered reliable year-round bloomers.

Lacy Leaves on Hollyhocks

Q: *Can you tell me what could be causing the leaves on my hollyhocks to turn yellow and look like lace— and what I can do to prevent it?*

A: There could be a combination of causes. "The most likely culprit is the Japanese beetle, which feeds on holly-hocks and skeletonizes the leaves. The beetles become active about July 1 in southern Michigan and continue feeding through August," says David Smitley, Ph.D., associate professor of entomology and Michigan State University extension specialist. Inspect the leaves of your plants regularly, armed with a solution of insecticidal soap. If you see munching beetles, squirt them and they will succumb. Hollyhock plants also are susceptible to rust, a fungus disease that causes leaves to turn yellow, wither, and drop early. Check the undersides of leaves for yellow or orange blisters that darken as they age. Eventually, similarly colored spots will appear on the top of the leaves. Remove and destroy the infected leaves; when flowering is over, collect all of the leaves and stalks and burn them, compost them, or dispose of them with the trash.

Bloomless Hydrangea

Q: *My hydrangea looks healthy, but it bloomed only the first summer. It hasn't bloomed for the past 5 years and I wonder why.*

A: 'Forever Pink' and other bigleaf hydrangeas (*Hydrangea macrophylla*) are not completely hardy in the North. Flower buds of this species form on the previous season's growth. When cold winters partially kill branch tips, few or no flowers form the following year.

Avoid overfertilizing, says Edmond Marrotte, consumer horticulturist at the University of Connecticut. Hydrangeas are light feeders. Too much nitrogen could halt bud production and increase the plant's susceptibility to winterkill.

Marrotte suggests visiting local nurseries and friends' yards to see what hydrangea varieties would do better in your area. White-flowered *Hydrangea paniculata* 'Grandiflora' is hardy to Zone 3 and is widely available.

Fast-Fading Impatiens

Q: *Last spring my impatiens germinated and grew fine early in the season. But as soon as the plants flowered, they died. They looked like they had been frozen. Can you help?*

A: There are several possible reasons for your fast-fading impatiens: lack of water, excessive sun, or plant disease. Let's take them one at a time.

"On a scale of 1 to 10, with 10 being the most water-loving, impatiens are 10s. They are usually the first plants to wilt in dry conditions," observes Ron Adams, technical service manager for Ball Horticulture Company in West Chicago, Illinois. In drought conditions, the lower leaves of impatiens turn yellow; eventually the entire plant shrivels up and dies.

Impatiens also do best in full to light shade. "They especially need shade between 10 A.M. and 2 P.M.," says Adams. But if you must choose between a site with morning sun and one with afternoon sun, give them the early sun. "Impatiens will wilt in the afternoon if you plant them on the west side of a house in full sun (even if they're getting enough water). If they get too much sun and not enough water, they can burn."

Of course, there's always the possibility that your plants succumbed to a fungal, bacterial, or viral disease. If your impatiens die again, consider sending a plant sample to the plant diagnostic lab at your state agricultural university. Pick up a form and instructions from your local county extension office (check the blue pages of your telephone book). If it turns out that you are dealing with a disease problem, ask your county extension office for resistant varieties suited to your area.

Ghostly Irises

Q: *Last year, all the colored irises in my main garden bloomed white. I trimmed them back last fall and fed them with bonemeal, and this year they bloomed white again! What is happening here? The irises growing in the horse pasture and along the drive all stayed true to color.*

A: "People accuse us of selling them trick 'color changing' irises all the time," says Tom Abrego, manager of Schreiner's Gardens, iris specialists, in Salem, Oregon. But contrary to popular misconception, "it's genetically impossible for such a color change to occur," he emphasizes. A more likely explanation is that you always had a few white irises in there, and they have now completely outcompeted the colored ones.

Did your main garden contain white irises that were especially vigorous? And did you fail to divide less vigorous colored varieties growing near them? "Less aggressive irises especially need to be divided every 4 years or so to flourish," says Abrego. "They don't like to get crowded." You can divide irises anytime in summer after they've finished blooming: Dig up crowded clumps, divide the rhizomes into smaller sections, making sure each has a growth "eye," and replant them about 1½ to 2 feet apart.

Lackadaisical Lilacs

Q: *My lilacs, which I've had for many years, have never bloomed. They're in acid soil, and the leaves have a grayish, powdery appearance.*

A: You may be growing the wrong lilac for your climate. Walter Oakes, secretary of the International Lilac Society, says the common lilac, *Syringa vulgaris*, doesn't flower well in warm climates. Lilac lovers south of Washington, D.C., may need to plant *S. hyacinthiflora*, which looks similar. Heard Gardens in Johnston, Iowa, offers several *S. hyacinthiflora* varieties and also recommends three *S. vulgaris* varieties for the South: 'Angel White', 'Blue Skies', and 'Lavender Lady' (see "Resources" on page 234).

Lilacs tolerate slightly acid or alkaline soils, but not extremes. And that grayish appearance is a harmless mildew that doesn't affect their ability to bloom.

Petal-Less Peonies

Q: *Why do my peonies fail to bloom, even though the plants appear green and healthy?*

A: Your peonies may fail to bloom even though the roots and tops look healthy for several reasons. If a close check reveals no sign of disease, then a late spring frost may have killed flower buds. If that's the case, your peonies should bloom this year (weather permitting, of course).

But a spring frost may not be the cause. To get the best blooms from peonies, be sure not to cut foliage back before it browns in the fall. And, remember that young plants, or divisions that have three or fewer eyes, will not bloom until they're older and larger.

Another common reason that peonies fail to bloom is that they have been planted too deeply. Crowns should be only 1 to 2 inches below the soil surface. Too much shade and poorly drained soil also will hinder blooming.

Additionally, plants that have been in place for decades and now are crowding each other or are losing growing space to tree and shrub roots will not bloom. If any of these are your growing site conditions, dig up your peonies and replant them elsewhere.

Prohibited Poppies?

Q: *I've seen opium poppy seed for sale only once—on an international seed exchange list. Is it illegal to grow it in the United States?*

A: Yes—the beautiful opium poppy (*Papaver somniferum*), also know as the breadseed poppy, is illegal to grow without a permit in the United States and Canada. But so many gardeners grow this plant anyway that it has escaped cultivation and also grows wild. Botanist James Duke, Ph.D., says he has seen *P. somniferum* varieties growing in home gardens in almost every state. Interestingly, it is only illegal to grow the plant; it's not illegal to sell or possess the seeds. Several U.S. seed companies currently offer *P. somniferum*, while several others offer various "breadseed poppy" varieties, which may or may not be *P. somniferum*.

And yes, the sap from the seedpods of this species is used to manufacture both illegal heroin and important legal pain-killing medications such as morphine and codeine. And yes, those same seedpods are also the source of the billions of tasty bluish gray poppy seeds used on rolls, cakes, and baked goods the world over.

The opium poppy is an upright annual with showy 3- to 4-inch, single or double flowers of white, pink, red, or purple. Dr. Duke says the poppy's seeds do not contain opium, although people who eat the seeds may test positive for illegal substances if they are subjected to drug testing.

Kill No Vine Before Its Time

Q: *I had a beautiful silver lace vine growing over my deck for 3 years, but last year it didn't survive a relatively mild winter. Why has my luck with this species run out? What could I plant in its place?*

A: "You probably killed it with kindness," says Michael Dirr, Ph.D., professor of ornamental horticulture at the University of Georgia in Athens and author of the *Manual of Woody Landscape Plants* (Stipes, 1998). "I've seen silver lace vine survive winters when temperatures dropped to -20°F. It's hard to kill."

Silver lace vine (*Polygonum aubertii*) thrives in dry soil and generally miserable conditions, and it grows where few vines have grown before. It's hardy from Zones 4 to 7 and grows fast—sometimes as much as 10 to 15 feet in one season. Your silver lace vine might not have hardened off enough to withstand winter temperatures (too much water or fertilizer could have been the culprit). If you want to try silver lace again, Dr. Dirr recommends fertilizing and watering it only enough to get it going in spring. Then just let it grow on its own without any more fussing.

If you've decided you've had enough of silver lace vine but miss the vine's late-summer and early-autumn blooms, try five-leaf akebia (*Akebia quinata*), cross vine (*Bignonia capreolata*), trumpet vine (*Campsis radicans or C. × tagliabuana* 'Mme. Galen'), sweet autumn clematis (*Clematis paniculata*), virgin's bower (*C. virginiana*)—"I've never seen anyone kill that one," Dr. Dirr says—or trumpet honeysuckle (*Lonicera sempervirens*).

Rusty Snapdragon

Q: *Despite planting in different locations, my snapdragons developed rust. How can I prevent this?*

A: Snapdragon rust (*Puccinia antirrhini*) is a common fungal disease that you can minimize through clean gardening practices and by growing rust-resistant varieties. Cool, humid weather encourages rust. Spores are spread by wind and splashing water, but foliage must remain wet for at least 6 hours for infection to occur. On infected plants, pale yellow spots appear on upper leaves and reddish brown pustules develop on the undersides. Severely affected plants have dried leaves, growth is stunted, and the plants die prematurely.

To minimize rust, water plants from underneath to keep foliage dry, suggests William Carlson, Ph.D., professor of plant physiology and floriculture at Michigan State University. Water in early morning to allow wet foliage to dry. Allow plenty of space between plants for good air circulation. Avoid high-nitrogen fertilizers. Destroy infected parts of plants, and remove all snapdragons at the end of the season to prevent spreading spores to new plantings the following season.

Sweet Alyssum Volunteers

Q: *Is there any reason I shouldn't use sweet alyssum in my vegetable garden? I had hundreds of alyssum volunteers last spring and thought about using them as a border around my vegetable garden. They seem to attract lots of beneficial insects, and I've also noticed that their trailing habit makes them an excellent weed-preventing mulch.*

A: Go right ahead and grow sweet alyssum (*Lobularia maritima*) throughout your garden. This tidy, low-growing annual flower is highly ornamental, perfumes the garden with its rich honey scent, makes a great living mulch, flowers early from direct seeding, and self-seeds easily but not excessively in future years. Alyssum is especially valuable because, as you've noticed, its flowers are highly attractive to beneficial insects, which are key to organic pest control.

To maximize the pest-control properties of sweet alyssum, be sure to plant this cold-hardy annual as early as possible, among any crops in which you've had aphid problems. Research at Colorado State and Oregon State Universities has confirmed that sweet alyssum's flowers are rich in nectar that attracts hoverflies, whose larvae feed on aphids inside tight places where other good bugs can't go. Hoverflies are especially helpful in early spring, when most other beneficials are not yet active.

TRICKY TECHNIQUES

Overwintering Dahlias

Q: *How can I overwinter dahlias in USDA Plant Hardiness Zone 2?*

A: After the first hard frost in fall, cut the main stems about 6 inches above ground level. Using a spading fork, gently loosen the soil about 1 foot away from the stem on all sides, then dig under the roots. Lift the clump carefully, drain moisture, and dry the clump in a cool, dry location. Clumps can be stored in a box in open air, vermiculite, or dry peat moss in a cool, dark area until spring.

Saving Potted Geraniums for Spring

Q: *How can I save my outdoor potted geraniums for replanting next spring?*

A: You can overwinter potted geraniums three different ways, according to Doc and Katy Abraham, garden writers from Naples, New York.

The first method is to remove the plants from their pots in the fall, before they get hit by frost, and hang them upside down by the roots in the cellar. Because most cellars (except those in old homes) are dry, wrap the plants in plastic bags with holes poked in the bags, and put a little moist peat in each bag. "It only takes a tiny amount of moisture to keep the plants alive over the winter," Doc Abraham says. Once or twice a month, wet a piece of rag or cotton ball, and slide it into each bag.

In February or March, take the plants down, soak them in a bucket of water for a half hour, cut the tops back, and pot them up in a mixture of equal parts sand, peat, and loam.

Another way to store the plants is to cut them back and put them (pot and all) in a tub of moist peat moss. Keep the tub in a bright window, and don't forget to give the geraniums a little water every once in a while. After the last frost in spring, set the plants outdoors. "You'll be surprised how fast those little 'sticks' perk up in spring," he says.

Or you can just keep the geraniums in their pots and grow them as houseplants over the winter. Geraniums like lots of light, so cut them back, and place them in a bright window, where the temperature stays around 55° to 60°F. Keep the soil moist. If the plants start to get leggy, cut the tops back. (You can root these cuttings, too.)

Yellow leaves indicate that the temperature is too high or the plant isn't getting enough light or water. When spring comes, trim the plants one more time, and set them outside.

Held Hostas

Q: *The hostas near the front entrance of my house are overrunning the sidewalk. How should I dig and divide them? I don't want to kill the plants or render them ugly for several years.*

A: The best time to thin out hostas to make them more manageable is in the early spring—just as the shoots are emerging from the ground. They can recover quickly during this stage and put out lots of new leaves afterward.

To divide, take a sharp spade or trowel, and cut out slices of roots from where the plants are too thick or too close to the sidewalk. Fill in any holes with fresh soil or compost, and use your newly acquired hosta roots to create a new bed of these shade-loving perennials elsewhere.

Lady's-Slipper Lore

Q: *In April, our wooded lot is polka-dotted with pink flowers that we call lady's-slippers, or wild orchids. Can we transplant them? What conditions would encourage them to bloom more?*

A: What you have on your land is the very beautiful native terrestrial orchid, *Cypripedium acaule*, which grows throughout most of the eastern United States. While this species is not officially on the endangered plant list, the plants are threatened by the loss of their natural habitat to development and the practice of "collection" by plant sellers who dig them up from the wild.

The plants rarely survive transplanting, however, because they require very specific growing conditions (the leafy, moldy duff of a forest floor) and have very shallow, brittle roots that are easily cracked and are thus prone to infection. "We usually discourage people from moving them," says Bill Cullina, nursery manager and propagator for the New England Wildflower Society in Framingham, Massachusetts. A plant may hang on for a year or two after it's moved, but usually it ends up dying, he says. "Better you leave them where they are and enjoy them there," he advises.

If you want more plants in their present location, try a little hand pollination. Use a toothpick to move some sticky yellow

When you think of hostas, you probably picture their stately foliage. Well, did you know that some hostas have wonderfully fragrant flowers, too? One of the best fragrant hostas is Hosta plantaginea, *also known as the August lily. Its trumpet-shaped flowers appear on bright green, 26-inch stems and fill the late summer and early autumn air with their delicious lilylike fragrance.*

pollen (found close to where the pouch attaches to the stem) to the female part of the flower (a moist spot at the opening of the pouch to which the pollen will adhere).

Then, to encourage flowers on nonblooming plants, give the plants more light. "They tend to bloom better if there's been some opening up of the [tree] canopy" by natural forces such as gypsy moths eating leaves, or ice storms breaking off tree branches, explains Cullina. "Remove some lower branches of surrounding plants, or thin out one or two thick trees to let in more dappled sunlight. It may take 1 or 2 years, but this usually triggers flowering."

Other than that, these plants like to be left to their own devices. "It's not necessary to water them unless there's a severe drought, and they don't need any extra mulch—pine needles would be OK—unless they are growing in a spot that's eroding. The more spartan the conditions, the better they can compete with other plants," says Cullina.

Woodland gardeners will probably do better with yellow lady's-slippers. These will grow in standard, moist, fertile garden soil, and their roots are not as prone to root rot, says Cullina. One source of yellow lady's-slippers is Spangle Creek Labs in Bovey, Minnesota (see "Resources" on page 234). "All our seedlings are grown from seed and do very well as long as our growing instructions are followed," states Carol Steele, co-owner.

Weed or Wildflower?

Q: *How and when should I dig up and transplant established wild Queen-Anne's-lace?*

A: Forget the digging. Queen-Anne's-lace is biennial: After it flowers in its second year, it's history. Although you *might* be able to move a 1-year plant, its long taproot would make this difficult. (This is a wild carrot, remember?) Besides, it's not conservationally correct to dig up wild plants, even one that flirts with being a weed, says Heather McCargo, a former plant propagator for the New England Wildflower Society. (Weed or not, organic gardeners know that lots of beneficial insects visit the flat, delicate flowers of Queen-Anne's-lace for pollen and nectar.)

The easiest way to domesticate Queen-Anne's-lace is to collect its seeds and sow them where you want the plant to grow. When the flower heads of second-year plants turn brown in late summer or fall, "run your hand across them, and if the seeds are ripe, they will come off in your hand," says McCargo.

"The seeds are not long-lived, so sow them right away in a row," she advises, "so you can tell whether they come up or not in spring—and don't cover them." If you must wait until spring to plant, store the seeds in an airtight jar in the refrigerator.

Here's more wildflower etiquette: Before you collect the seed of a wild plant, always get the landowner's permission, advises McCargo. Make sure the plant is properly identified and common where you found it—not on an endangered species list. "And never take more than 5 percent of the seed that's available in that little spot," she says.

Chapter

3

FRUIT

Fruit you've grown yourself is sinfully delicious—fresh, juicy, and sweet—perfect for dressing up a dessert or eating plain. Growing fruit can be a little challenging, though. Read on to learn the answers to common fruit-growing questions such as when to prune raspberries and how to grow apples organically.

GENERAL CARE
Fruit Protection

Q: *We have 2 acres of fruit trees, all facing south. Each year the trees bloom early and full and then get destroyed by a late frost. Apples, prunes, and sour cherries usually survive, but in the past 5 years, we haven't harvested one peach, nectarine, apricot, pear, plum, or sweet cherry.*

A: David Lockwood, Ph.D., extension fruit specialist at the University of Tennessee, says you can do several things. First, be sure your trees are as healthy as possible so they can better withstand the cold. Trees under stress from lack of nutrients or an abundance of pests also tend to bloom a little earlier.

If any fencerows have grown up on the slope below the orchard, cut them down to increase the airflow down from the orchard site, Dr. Lockwood advises. (Frost tends to settle in low or still areas.) Keep the orchard and downhill areas fairly clean of tall weeds—these can also slow down air movement. So can low-hanging limbs. Prune these to improve airflow among your trees.

Be sure to prune apple and pear trees when they're dormant because fire-blight infection from a pruning cut increases in the spring. But don't prune the others until most danger of frost has passed. And when you do prune, try not to remove a lot of the higher branches, which hold the buds and flowers that are most likely to survive a frost. Then if frost does occur, just prune out the damaged branches.

Of course, some fruit varieties are hardier than others and yours may not be the best trees for your area. Discuss this with your county extension agent.

Summer Pruning for More Fruit

Q: *I've heard of something called the Lorette summer pruning method that keeps fruit trees small but productive in gardens with limited space. Can you give me any information on how to do this or suggest any books or publications on the subject?*

A: The Lorette system of pruning (named after a turn-of-the-century French horticulturist) is best suited to pear and apple varieties that aren't too vigorous. It works especially well if you want to grow dwarf trees into long horizontal or vertical cordon shapes or flat espaliers against a wall.

Basically, the Lorette system consists of cutting off succulent new shoots as soon as they are about 12 inches long and the thickness of a pencil and a cluster of three to five leaves has sprouted at the base of the shoot. The cuts are made very close (¼ to ⅜ inch) to the base of the shoot.

Unlike "dormant pruning," which is done in winter (or early spring before the tree's leaves begin to grow), this *summer* pruning doesn't stimulate branching or vigorous growth. Instead, the tree forms fruiting spurs directly on its thicker branches where the vegetative shoots were removed.

Cut off the shoots promptly so as not to drain too much of the tree's energy. "In trees that grow vigorously, you might have to do this cutting a number of times in early summer to get the desired effect," notes Brad Taylor, Ph.D., associate professor of plant and soil sciences at Southern Illinois University. And don't prune after Labor Day, or the late-in-the-season new growth you'll cause won't have time to toughen

up before winter. Basic structural pruning should still be done in the dormant season, when it's easier to see the limb structure of the tree, he continues.

We found a good explanation of the Lorette pruning system in that bible of pomology, *Dwarfed Fruit Trees* by Harold Bradford Tukey (Cornell University Press, 1978). Your local public library can obtain a copy for you to borrow. They may also be able to rustle up a copy of *The Lorette System of Pruning* by Louis Lorette himself, translated from the French and first published in England in 1925 and reprinted in 1946. Sadly, this book is now out of print, but library copies *are* out there.

Whitewashing for Winter Sunscald

Q: *What is the recipe for whitewash to paint the trunks of my fruit trees?*

A: No real "recipe"—just use white latex interior paint to protect your fruit trees from sunscald during the winter. It's important that you use interior paint, not exterior—interior paint doesn't have all the solvents that exterior paint does—and also be sure you use latex, which is water-based.

Sunscald may sound like a summertime peril, but it's actually a cold-weather problem. Winter sun warms up the tender bark on the southern surface of trees, much more than bark on the northern surface. Then, when the sun ducks behind a cloud or sets, the surface temperature quickly drops, and the sudden change causes the bark to split open. Bacteria or insects may enter the splits and cause further damage. The light color of the whitewash reflects the sun's rays and prevents those dangerous sudden temperature changes.

Stephen Page, coauthor of *The Orchard Almanac—A Seasonal Guide to Healthy Fruit Trees* (AgAccess Publications, 1996) does have a recipe of sorts in that he prefers to water the paint down a bit. He adds 2 parts paint to 1 part water, so that the paint goes a little farther. On a warm November or December day in his Searsmont, Maine, orchard, he coats the south and southwest sides right up to the lower tier of branches. "I even paint some of the lower branches because they can get sunscald, too," he adds.

Page also paints a 6-inch band all the way around the base of the trunk to make it easier to monitor the presence of apple tree borers. He checks the trunks every 2 weeks during the growing season and "grubs" out any borers by working a piece of wire up the hole they've made.

BERRIES & MELONS

Alpine Strawberry Care

Q: *Is the care and propagation of alpine strawberries different from that of regular strawberries?*

A: Native to northern Eurasia, alpine strawberries produce smaller fruits on smaller plants over a longer harvest season than modern strawberries. Their total yield is less, however. Given rich soil, full sun, and a steady supply of water, alpine strawberries grow and fruit easily. They're well suited for garden beds, borders, and containers and even as a groundcover.

Alpine strawberries don't throw many runners, but you can propagate them by either seed, runners, or divisions of mature plants. If you want to divide, encourage more roots on side crowns by mounding soil over the base of the plant in late summer or early fall. After the ground has frozen, mulch plants with 3 to 6 inches of straw. (You don't need to cut

back the plants.) Remove the mulch just before plant growth resumes in spring. When new growth starts, dig the plants, cut apart the well-rooted sections, and replant.

Several varieties of alpine strawberries are available to American gardeners. Beginning alpine strawberry gardeners might try 'Alexandria', which is a standard European variety and is available from Johnny's Selected Seeds (see "Resources" on page 234).

Exploding Melons

Q: *Two years ago I planted 'Ambrosia' cantaloupes. Just a couple days short of maturity, the blossom end of every melon exploded open like a trumpet. This summer, I planted 'Savor' (a Charantais melon) in the same plot of ground. The plants were very healthy and the melons had attained a bluish rind and beautiful orange flesh but were still very firm when they also all exploded. I've grown melons in this garden for many years and never had such a problem until recently.*

A: Sounds like moisture stress, say our experts, who wonder what the weather was like while your melons were growing. Ray Rothenberger, Ph.D., professor of horticulture at the University of Missouri, says that a long spell of dry weather followed by lots of rain can cause slowly developing fruit to put on a big spurt of growth that could cause such splitting.

Brent Loy, Ph.D., a cantaloupe breeder and a professor of plant biology at the University of New Hampshire, adds that if your muggy nights stayed over 70°F consistently, the weather could have made your melons grow too fast and compounded the problem. Next time, choose a long-season, slow-growing melon, and mulch your plants heavily to keep their moisture supply nice and even. Dr. Loy adds that Charantais melons such as 'Savor' are supposed to be picked before the stem slips off and while they are still slightly hard. "They will turn to mush if they are still on the vine at maturity," he warns.

Cutting Canes

Q: *After I cut my 'Heritage' raspberry plants down to the ground last spring, I had a groundcover of raspberry plants—hundreds of them. I'm getting ready to cut them again—how do I tell which ones are the originals, and how do I get rid of the rest?*

A: If you cut your 'Heritage' raspberry plants to ground level, it doesn't matter which canes are the original and which are the new ones, says Mary Jo Kelly, technician in the fruit and vegetable science department at Cornell University. "You want to keep them all," unless you need to remove some to make manageable rows.

When you cut everbearing raspberries down to the ground in late winter (or early spring) to save pruning time, you lose that first, early summer crop; each cane will be a "primocane" that will bear only a late crop. If you don't cut them all down, you should prune off the spent (wooden) part of canes that produced fruit last year. It is, however, these older canes that bear the early crop, which is smaller—but not always—than the late one. You should not cut down all the canes of summer-bearing varieties, such as 'Titan' or 'Newburgh', or you won't get any crop. Summer-bearing raspberries fruit only on 2-year-old canes.

Rotten Raspberries

Q: *Help! Our 'Heritage' raspberries died from root rot after just 2 years of harvests. Are there varieties that can better tolerate our heavy-clay soil?*

A: "No raspberry variety is totally immune to root rot (*Phytophthora*), says Wayne Wilcox, Ph.D., a plant pathologist who specializes in fungal diseases at Cornell University. "But some varieties are less susceptible than others."

'Amity', a fall-bearing red raspberry released by Oregon State University in Corvallis and the Washington Agricultural Research Center in Pullman, is less susceptible to root rot than most other varieties. It begins to mature in mid-August, about 5 days before 'Heritage' in the Corvallis area. 'Amity' is available from Park Seed in Greenwood, South Carolina and 'Heritage' from Bear Creek Nursery in Northport, Washington (see "Resources" on page 234 for addresses).

"Anything you can do to improve soil drainage also will help prevent root rot," says Dr. Wilcox. "Incorporate organic matter into the soil and plant new raspberries in raised mounds, but avoid low-lying areas." Don't plant new raspberries in the same area as the infected plants for at least 2 years. You can plant other crops in the interim.

Wilting canes, stunted growth, and chlorotic leaves all indicate root rot. To confirm root rot, dig up a piece of the root and scrape off the top layer of bark. Healthy roots appear white; infected roots look reddish brown. What gardeners sometimes call winter dieback—wilting and dying of cane tips in spring—often is also due to root rot.

White Spots on Red Raspberries

Q: *Why do small sections on my red raspberries remain white when they're ripe?*

A: Sounds like your red raspberries are suffering from a case of sunburn. "We get very hot weather that bleaches, or whitens, the berries," says Chad Finn, state fruit crops specialist at the University of Missouri. Those small sections you refer to are called drupelets; a single raspberry is composed of many drupelets. The solar injury that causes individual drupelets to whiten and become hard and shriveled is common in the South at higher elevations and on the east side of north-south rows.

Finn recommends your shading berries when they start to turn red (set up a shade cloth or similar material over the bushes). Some growers use water sprinklers to cool their berries and prevent sunburn, but the air has to be dry for the water to evaporate and cooling to take place.

If you're starting a new planting, he recommends fall-bearing raspberries such as 'Heritage', 'Redwing', or other berries that start bearing in mid-August and later. "You won't avoid the problem completely, but you will reduce bleaching because most of the crop will mature when the sun is not as intense."

Diseased Strawberries

Q: *The leaves of our strawberries developed small purple spots but looked healthy otherwise. Is this something we should worry about?*

A: "It's probably leaf scorch," says Stephen Ries, Ph.D., plant pathologist and extension fruit specialist at the University of Illinois. Purple spots with white centers indicate leaf spot, another common fungal disease on strawberries. Both diseases usually appear in July or August during hot, humid seasons. Depending on the fertility of your patch, affected plant crowns could be weakened enough to reduce fruit yield 10 to 20 percent the following season, says Dr. Ries.

Dr. Ries advises renovating the patch immediately after harvest to remove most of the disease inoculum. Mow the entire planting with the lawn-mower blade set high to cut off leaves, where most of the pathogen is located. New tissue will be relatively free of the fungus. In fall, till between plants to create 12- to 14-inch rows. Dense plantings promote fungal diseases because leaves cannot dry.

Even cultivars such as 'Late Glow', which has resistance to leaf scorch and leaf spot, could become infected during unusually hot, humid conditions. Try the above cultural controls before replanting with new varieties, says Philip Ahrens, owner of Ahrens Strawberry Nursery in Huntingburg, Indiana.

TREE & VINE FRUITS

A Raking a Day Keeps Apple Scab Away

Q: *My county agent tells me that I can control apple scab only by spraying with chemicals. Is there an organic way to control this disease?*

A: Maybe your county agent should talk to Steve Johnson at the Lazy J Tree Farm in Port Angeles, Washington. Johnson has several acres of organic apples, and he prevents scab by raking up the tree's leaves, then tilling any he missed into the surface of his orchard to keep it as clean as possible, followed by sulfur sprays and foliar feeds.

Rake up old apple leaves, dried-up apples, and twigs, and get rid of them. Bury them or compost them; just take them far away from your apple trees—scab overwinters on this kind of surface debris, then moves back to the tree when buds open in spring. (So if you do compost the debris, don't use the compost around your apple trees.)

Fungicidal sprays such as sulfur or lime-sulfur are tricky to use and can cause leaf damage if applied incorrectly. Newer liquid sulfur emulsions are easier and safer, but if apples aren't your livelihood, try to rely on scrupulous sanitation instead.

The best and easiest organic scab control is to plant resistant varieties, such as 'Williams Pride', 'Redfree', 'Dayton', 'Novamac', 'Jonafree', 'Freedom', 'Liberty', 'Nova Easygro', 'Sir Prize', and 'MacFree'.

Don't forget to give your apples adequate water and nutrition. Irrigate when rainfall is light and spread at least 2 inches of compost beneath each tree annually. Treat your trees to a seaweed spray when buds begin to show color, repeat after the petals fall, and then spray again when young fruits are ½ to 1 inch in diameter.

The Organic Apple Challenge

Q: *I am having a running argument with a neighbor who insists that you cannot grow a good apple without spraying toxic chemicals on the tree. Can you provide some information on how to manage an organic apple orchard? (My neighbor has given me the opportunity to prove my point by letting me take care of several old apple trees in his back field!) Also, our community has several "pick-your-own" apple orchards, and I'd like information and statistics so that I can approach them about "greening up" their practices.*

A: Your neighbor's offer sounds like a setup. Do you know exactly what kind of apples your neighbor has? Certain varieties are difficult to grow organically, especially in New England, which has certain pests and diseases that other areas don't. To grow blemish-free organic apples in your region,

CHECK IT OUT!

Indeed, apples can be a challenge to grow organically because many varieties are susceptible to disease. But apple breeders are making great progress in developing disease-resistant varieties. Two examples are 'Enterprise', a late red apple, and 'Gold Rush', an even later yellow variety. 'Enterprise' is highly resistant to apple scab, cedar apple rust, and fire blight. Crispy, tart 'Gold Rush' is highly resistant to apple scab and powdery mildew. Both varieties are available from Stark Brothers Nursery (see "Resources" on page 234).

you'll need to use red sticky traps and hope that your neighbor's trees are scab-resistant varieties such as 'Redfree' or 'Liberty'.

Now, despite those cautions, the truth is that you can grow any apple organically—it's just that some years you'll have better quality fruit than others, explains Terry Schettini, director of horticulture at the Rodale Institute Experimental Farm in Maxatawny, Pennsylvania, where organic apple orchard production is continually studied. Factors that will affect the quality include the weather, where the apple trees are located in relation to other apple trees (or alternate hosts of apple pests), and year-to-year cycles of disease and insect pressure. (For example, Schettini explains that if your apple trees are near a stand of cedar trees, they may be susceptible to cedar apple rust, a fungus disease. And other conditions—like the weather—could make that problem worse some years and keep it under control in others.)

Of course, it's impossible to fully answer your requests in the limited space we have here. So Sarah Wolfgang Heffner, former orchard project manager at the Rodale Farm, has the following advice: "Contact your local extension agent and join your local organic farming association to find out who else is growing apples in your area and what the pest issues are because problems and solutions are often very location-specific. And get in touch with the North American Fruit Explorers, a good organization for people interested in growing fruit." (See "Resources" on page 234.)

Books and guides are also available to help you. Sarah especially likes the little directory of sources for organic materials, tools, and beneficial insects put together by *Organic Gardening* magazine. (Contact *Organic Gardening*, 33 E. Minor Street, Emmaus, PA 18098, for how to obtain the "Organic Supplies" brochure.) Her favorite books for organic fruit growing are *The Apple Grower—A Guide for the Organic Orchardist* by Michael Phillips (Chelsea Green Publishing,

1998), and *The Orchard Almanac—A Seasonal Guide to Healthy Fruit Trees* by Stephen Page and Joe Smillie (AgAccess Publications, 1996).

Margaret Christie, grower coordinator for the Sustainable Apple Production Project, suggests "The Real Dirt: Farmers Tell about Organic and Low-Input Practices in the Northeast" by Miranda Smith (available from Vermont Northeast Organic Farming Association, P.O. Box 697, Richmond, VT 05477; (802) 434-4122). Another organization you might find helpful is Backyard Fruit Growers, 817 High Street, Akron, PA 17501-1417. The organization has seasonal meetings and publishes a quarterly newsletter.

Apple-Less Tree

Q: *We have two old 'Delicious' apple trees on our property. For the first time in the 10 years we've lived here, one bore heavily while the other had no fruit. Both usually produce plenty of fruit. The tree that bore no fruit looks healthy otherwise. Is it normal for this to happen?*

A: If your trees are 'Red Delicious', it's possible that one of them had a pollination problem, limiting fruit set. This could have been caused by a late spring freeze or cool rainy weather, explains Chris Walsh, Ph.D., professor of horticulture at the University of Maryland.

How could this be possible, you ask, when they are *both* the same kind of apple? They probably aren't, says Dr. Walsh. "There are many varieties that look very similar to 'Red Delicious'," he explains. 'Red Virginia Winesap', for instance, looks like 'Red Delicious' but is more prone to pollination problems. Or one of your trees could be a *grafted* 'Red Delicious' and the other one could be a *seedling* (ungrafted) 'Red Delicious'. The grafted tree would have a completely different root system and thus could respond very differently to the weather, says Dr. Walsh.

And if you have 'Golden Delicious' trees, it's possible that one was just falling into its natural habit of bearing every other year. In fact, *all* apples once had a tendency to bear fruit only every other year; a trait that has been bred out of most modern varieties.

Apple Storage Success Secrets

Q: *We harvest beautiful apples, but the ones we store in our dry, cool basement shrivel and rot over the winter. How can we store these apples successfully?*

A: Sounds like the temperature in your basement is all right, but the humidity is not. Unless the humidity is around 90 percent, apples will shrivel. They also need an optimal temperature of 30° to 32°F—just 10° warmer and they'll ripen twice as fast.

If you have a small batch of apples, a refrigerator or basement is probably the best way to store them. If your basement isn't cold enough, try storing your apples in insulated containers in an unheated building or outside in straw-lined pits.

For larger amounts of apples, you may want to set up a humidifier in the basement, says W. C. Stiles, Ph.D., an apple researcher at Cornell University. You can make your own "humidifier" by walling off a small area and hanging up burlap so that the bottom end dips into a pan of water, with a fan set up right behind the burlap sheet to blow the moist air throughout the cellar. Just remember, though, that the motor of the fan (or a regular humidifier) will give off heat—and may be enough to warm up your apples.

Dr. Stiles also recommends that you line your apple storage containers with perforated plastic liners to help prevent the apples from drying out. Be sure to poke holes in the plastic to allow *some* air circulation even if your liner is just a plastic bag.

He also stresses the importance of careful handling. Any bruises or breaks in the skin could lead to decay once the apple is in storage. Be sure stored apples are hard, mature, and in *perfect* condition; apples picked too green could develop scald or bitter pit in storage, and overripe apples will rot no matter what you do. Cool the apples as quickly as possible after harvest, and be sure to check your apple stash regularly for rotten fruit—one bad apple *will* spoil the whole bunch.

Although apples generally store well (compared to a lot of other fruits), keeping quality does vary among varieties. The better keepers are generally the late-maturing varieties, Dr. Stiles says. If you have a choice, go with 'Granny Smith' (in the South or West), which is one of the best keepers (sometimes lasting up to 6 months). 'Winesap', 'Rome Beauty', 'Northern Spy', 'Melrose', and 'Idared' are also good choices.

Wanted Grapes, Got Raisins

Q: *For the past two years, our six seedless grapevines have had a blight and the fruit turned into inedible raisins before harvest. What can we do to prevent this?*

A: It sounds like your grapes have black rot. John Peplinski, Ph.D., coordinator of the plant disease clinic at Penn State University, says this disease is caused by a fungus that overwinters in shriveled-up grapes that were left on the vines or that have fallen to the ground. In spring, fungal spores from these mummified fruits are splashed by rain or carried by wind to the plants, where they cause leaf spots and infect the new fruit.

Dispose of diseased fruit immediately by burying it away from the vines so the fungal spores can't spread. Cultivate lightly around your vines to bury any black rot spores on the soil's surface. Some growers plant thick cover crops that keep spores on the soil from traveling back to the vines.

Eliminate any wild grapes or Boston ivy in the vicinity of your grape arbor—if infected, these plants can spread it to your grapes, Dr. Peplinski says.

Fruitless Kiwis

Q: *We've had monster vines for more than 8 years, but no fruit from our hardy kiwis. We have at least two males. The plants are growing in clay on a well-drained slope.*

A: Hardy kiwifruit, the common name for *Actinidia arguta*, generally takes 3 to 9 years to reach first blossom or sexual maturity, depending on how much heat the soil around the root system retains in your specific microclimate, explains "Kiwi Bob" Glanzman, the Kiwi Interest Group coordinator for the North American Fruit Explorers. Vigorous vines without blossoms indicate the plants have sufficient moisture and nutrients, but the root system isn't receiving enough heat to initiate first bloom. In that case, be patient—the plants may still bloom during the next few years. If they don't bloom by the time they're 15 years old, however, they never will. If that happens, plant your next vines in a partially shaded spot, but where the roots will get more sun.

It's also possible that your plants produced a few blossoms that didn't result in fruit. "Both male and female plants need to bloom before you will get fruit," explains Glanzman. Perhaps your plants were mislabeled. Look closely at the flowers the next time they bloom. On male kiwis, the flowers have only stamens, while the flowers on female and self-fertile kiwis have both stamens and pistils. If you have only male or only female vines, get a new vine of the missing sex.

Pruning may also affect blossoming. All kiwi flowers emerge from leaf nodes on the current season's new vine growth, coming from the previous year's 1-year-old wood. New shoots may emerge from 2-year-old or older wood, but they won't have any blossoms. When you prune, leave 8 to 12 leaf nodes of the most recent vine growth on each remaining branch to generate the next year's blossoming wood.

For more helpful advice, contact the North American Fruit Explorers, a nonprofit organization of backyard fruit-growing enthusiasts. For membership information, write to 1716 Apples Road, Chapin, IL 62628. You can also visit their Web site at www.nafex.org.

Quick Kiwi Quiz

Q: *For the first time in 4 or 5 years, my hardy kiwi plants are bearing. The fruit is in clusters. Should I thin them? How should I prune and when? Can I propagate hardy kiwi plants by burying the leaders?*

A: OK, first, there is no need to thin clusters of hardy kiwi fruits, assures our expert, Daniel Milbocker, Ph.D., professor of horticulture at the Hampton Roads Agricultural Research Station in Virginia Beach, Virginia.

But it is important, he explains, to prune your *vine*—long before those clusters appear, so that when the vine later becomes loaded with fruit, it doesn't hit the ground, where it can rot and/or be eaten by creatures other than you.

"Prune your kiwi vines as if they were grapevines," says Dr. Milbocker. First, train the main stem of the vine onto a trellis and allow two main branches to grow each way from the main stem over the supports. Side branches will sprout from these two main branches. Cut the side branches back so that there are four and eight buds between the cut and the main branch (fruit is borne on new growth, and these buds will sprout into fruit-bearing wood). While you're at it, prune off any dead wood, too. Then in summer, as the side branches grow (they can grow 10 to 14 feet in a season), remove any that are causing problems by intertwining with their neighbors.

You should do this pruning at a specific time: in late winter, after the danger of *deep* winter frost has passed, but before warm spring weather starts the sap flowing inside the vines.

And, yes, it is possible—even easy—to grow new vines from old by layering (burying a portion of a vine) because roots will form where a vine comes in contact with the soil. In fact, "the hardy kiwi species tends to root quite readily," assures Stephen Breyer, kiwi nurseryman and owner of Tripple Brook Farm in Southampton, Massachusetts.

To perform such propagation, select a slender vine with smaller leaves. Bury a short length of the vine, about 6 inches to 1 foot from the tip, a couple inches deep, and use a brick or rock to hold it in place. Choose a location in bright light but not direct sunlight, and water the buried portion of vine occasionally if the weather is dry, says Breyer.

After roots begin to sprout from the buried section of vine, just cut the connection to the main plant, and you've got brand new kiwi plant!

"Make sure the new plant is well rooted by cautiously poking around," says Breyer. (*Hint:* If you bury your vine in a *pot* of soil, you won't have to dig up the new plant to move it to another location—just be sure to keep it from drying out.)

Lemons Like Consistency

Q: *I bought a 'Meyer' lemon tree to grow in a container a few years ago and the first year I got three incredible lemons. For the last couple years, though, I've had four flushes of fragrant blossoms followed by baby lemons that fell off the tree before they were 1 inch long. I keep the tree in a sunny window during the winter and outside in summer. It gets compost a couple times a year and a good watering twice a week when it's hot. What am I doing wrong?*

A: "It's to be expected that some of the fruit will drop as the tree thins itself. However, when all the fruit falls off, it's usually due to stress caused by too little water or irregular watering. In addition, that sunny window may provide too much heat," says Don Dillon Jr., third generation owner of Four Winds Growers of Dwarf Citrus in Fremont, California.

Unlike some other citrus, "'Meyer' lemons don't need direct sun," he continues. "When the fruit is tiny, keep your tree out of intense light and keep the soil moist—the fruit should stay and grow bigger."

More advice: Water the plant at least three times a week in high heat. And besides applying compost, feed your tree monthly with a liquid fish fertilizer and seaweed solution. "Citrus trees are heavy feeders and like trace elements such as copper, iron, magnesium, and zinc," says Dillon.

Don Dillon Sr., co-proprietor of Four Winds Growers, offers the following general citrus advice: "These trees appreciate gentle treatment and consistent conditions. Always provide easy drainage, and keep the soil moist. Avoid extremes—don't drown them, dry them out, or fry them. But don't mother them to death, either. A nice, calm demeanor should help—they are really quite resilient and appreciative of little favors."

Moldy Peaches

Q: *A mold grows on my peaches just as they ripen. Is there something I can do to prevent this?*

A: The mold is probably brown rot, which is caused by the fungus *Monilinia fructicola*. The disease spreads from infected fruit, says Stephen Page, coauthor of *The Orchard Almanac— A Seasonal Guide to Healthy Fruit Trees*, an excellent book on growing fruit organically (AgAccess Publications, 1996).

To reduce the occurrence of brown rot next season, collect and destroy all the infected fruits you can find this season. Collect immature, mummified fruits as soon as you spot them—whether on the tree or the ground.

Destroy the diseased fruits by placing them in a very hot, active compost pile or by burying them. "You could also ferment them," says Page. "Put the infected fruit in a plastic bag, seal it tight, and set it in a sunny spot." Prune the tree, and trim back surrounding plants to improve air circulation because moist conditions help spread the disease, too.

Pears Won't Ripen

Q: *Although I've picked them and wrapped them in newspaper, my 'Bartlett' pears stay hard and green long after the ripening date for our zone. What's wrong?*

A: "'Bartlett' pears should begin to show some ripening on the tree by the end of August in your area of the Southwest," says Joe Preczewski, product development manager for Stark Bro's Nurseries in Louisiana, Missouri. "First, positively identify the fruit to be sure that you actually have a 'Bartlett'. Nurseries sometimes make mistakes and mislabel the varieties." If you verify that it is a 'Bartlett', improper handling after harvest could be the problem.

"With pears, the number-one problem for home growers is handling," Preczewski says. "Harvest fall pears when fruit color begins to lighten—with 'Bartlett', that's usually late August in your area." Generally, fruit also softens slightly at maturity, except during a hot, dry season, when mature fruit tends to be yellow but firm. In cool seasons, mature pears tend to be softer and greener than those grown in hot, dry conditions.

"Most varieties should be refrigerated immediately after picking. It isn't necessary to wrap them in newspaper," advises Preczewski. "After 7 to 10 days at cool temperatures, finish ripening fruit at 65° to 70°F, or room temperature. Pears should soften and yellow."

Where Did All the Plums Go?

Q: *I have a 5-year-old plum tree in my small garden. The tree was full of fruit its second and third year, but it failed to bear any the following years. Could it be that I pruned the tree the wrong way or at the wrong time?*

A: It's difficult to misprune a plum tree. "You would have had to remove *all* the fruit buds to have no fruit," says Anna Flory of Hilltop Nurseries, L.L.C., fruit tree specialists in Hartford, Michigan. Here's her pruning advice, just in case: In late winter when the tree is dormant, open up the tree just a little bit by removing some of the biggest upright shoots. *Don't* remove the "fruiting spurs"—the smaller, short branches on 2- to 4-year-old wood—because "you will get lots of fruit production on these smaller branches," she explains.

Now back to what could have gone wrong for you. If your tree didn't *bloom* at *all,* cold winter temperatures may have killed all the fruit buds, proposes Flory. If the tree *bloomed* but still produced no fruit, "the most logical probability is that the open flowers were subjected to freezing temperatures, died, and so didn't set fruit," suggests Warren Smith, an agent with the Cornell Cooperative Extension of Ulster County, New York. Erratic spring weather often causes such troubles, he adds.

And what about pollination? Is your tree one of the varieties that needs a pollinator (another plum tree) growing nearby to produce pollen to fertilize its blossoms? If so, where is that pollinator?

Or did you perchance overfertilize the tree? The experts we consulted all warn that too much nitrogen can cause a tree to grow more leaves and fewer flowers. A rich mulch of compost mixed with a little aged manure should be all the fertilizer your plum tree needs.

Black Plum Plague

Q: We've lost several plum trees to black knot disease. Is there something we can do to save the rest of the trees? Are there any resistant varieties?

A: Black knot is a fungal disease that causes rough, dark swellings (knots) to form on the twigs and branches of infected trees. After overwintering in infected wood, fungal spores shoot into the air during spring rains, spreading the infection to other nearby plum trees. To prevent more damage to your trees, inspect them often, especially in late winter before buds form, and prune away infected wood. Cut at least 2 to 4 inches below each knot—the fungus grows beyond the edge of the knot itself. Bury or burn the prunings.

Are there old or abandoned plum trees in your area? Wild plums and wild cherry trees can carry the disease, too. Get rid of any nearby wild trees that show symptoms if you can.

'President', a late-maturing European plum with blue-black skin and yellow flesh, is resistant, say the pathologists at

Cornell's New York State Agricultural Experiment Station. 'Early Italian' has *some* tolerance. Both are available from Van Well Nursery in Wenatchee, Washington (see "Resources" on page 234).

Secrets of Ripe Watermelons

Q: *Why weren't my 'Dixie Queen' watermelons ripe at 90 days? And once they did ripen, why did half the crop have cracks in the flesh?*

A: Watermelons are heat-loving, and cool weather will push their ripening date beyond those numbers on the seed package. So depending on where you live, some crops may take longer than expected to mature.

If you want to grow long-season watermelons, try 'Jubilee' or 'Crimson Sweet', says Bernard Zandstra, Ph.D., an extension vegetable specialist at Michigan State University. Some varieties are more prone to interior cracks, or "hollow heart," than others. Too much water or nitrogen can also lead to hollow heart.

Determining exactly when a watermelon is ripe is one of the ultimate gardening questions—and talents. First, look for a gray, dull film on the outside rather than a shiny green gloss. Next, see if the tendril nearest the point on the vine where the fruit stem attaches is brown or dead. Check if the spot where the fruit rests on the ground is yellow. If the answer to any of these questions is yes, then proceed to how the watermelon sounds. When you flick it with your fingers, you should hear a hollow, resounding "punk," as opposed to a "pink" or a "pank." From a Japanese watermelon breeder: When it sounds like thumping your forehead, it's still green; when it sounds like thumping your chest, it's ripe; and when it sounds like thumping your stomach, it's overripe.

Chapter

4

HERBS, SPICES & NUTS

Herbs, spices, or nuts all come in
handy when you need to add a little (or
a lot) of something to dress up a dish.
They also come with their own sets of
questions, such as why your dittany of
Crete plant won't bloom, how to overwinter rosemary, and how to grow and
harvest pistachios. Turn the page to
find the answers.

113

HERBS

Windowsill Herbs

Q: *I live in a small apartment and would like to grow herbs on my kitchen windowsill. What are the best varieties to grow in small containers?*

A: You can grow almost *any* herb on a windowsill, as long as you trim the plants often to keep them nice and bushy and compact. But some herbs are especially suited to windowsill growing, says Louise Hyde of Well-Sweep Herb Farm in Port Murray, New Jersey. "'Italian' oregano, for instance, stays less than 10 inches tall and has a very good flavor," she says, adding that "we also like to grow our 'Logee Blue' rosemary indoors because it's less subject to fungus than some other rosemaries. It has a beautiful dark blue flower and grows to only about 10 inches tall in the house."

A couple of small basils are also good for growing indoors, she continues. "'Miniature' (*Ocimum basilicum minimum*), the smallest basil, grows only 6 to 8 inches tall; and 'Globe' forms a roundish little bush less than 1 foot tall. English and lemon thyme do well indoors, too, growing thick and full as you clip them. Regular curly leaf parsley and sage will also thrive in the house," she adds, "and if they get too big, just nip them back."

Carol Lacko-Beem, owner of Herbs-Liscious in Iowa, points out that bay laurel is also a good house herb. Even though it *is* a small tree in its native climate, it grows very slowly in a pot, she explains. One herb *not* suited to windowsill growing, however, is tarragon—it needs a period of chilling.

Hyde offers these general indoor herb growing tips: "Plant herb seedlings in 4-inch-wide containers—a good size for most windowsills—filled with a good potting soil—not dirt from your garden. Fertilize the plants (compost tea or a seaweed spray) every 6 to 8 weeks, but hold back a little in winter when the plants grow very slowly. Give indoor herbs as much sun or light as possible—cleaning their window on both sides makes a *big* difference. And keep them on the dry side—water only when the top of the soil feels dry."

Dittany of Crete

Q: *Can you tell me why my dittany of Crete plants won't bloom?*

A: "Dittany of Crete" (*Origanum dictamnus*) will bloom in midsummer if given bright light and dry soil—conditions that resemble its native Mediterranean habitat. To encourage your plants to produce their delicate pink flowers, keep them in a southern window, says Tovah Martin of Logee's Greenhouses in Danielson, Connecticut, a supplier of dittany (see "Resources" on page 234). Amend regular potting soil with sand to provide good drainage, or use cactus potting soil. Allow the soil to dry completely between waterings. Gardeners who live in arid regions can move the plants outdoors for the summer. Expect the plants to drop some of their foliage when blossoming begins.

Unlike other members of the oregano family, dittany of Crete is not used in cooking. Ancient Greeks used the herb medicinally; its downy, silver leaves were reputed to heal wounds. According to folklore, Greek hunters believed that wounded goats rolled in dittany would heal.

Bland Oregano

Q: *We noticed that our oregano lost its aroma and flavor when I tried to dry it. What varieties do you recommend for successful drying?*

A: Classic oregano belongs to a big, wide-ranging family of herbs. Both seeds and plants sold as oregano are often the more generic *Origanum vulgare*, which might not have the flavor you need to spice up your pizza.

The oregano you want is *O. heracleoticum.* But all the oreganos cross-pollinate readily, and seeds may not produce a plant with the kind of oregano flavor you want. To achieve the flavor you crave, start with a plant of the desired species. Plants of *O. heracleoticum* are available from Companion Plants, 7247 N. Coolville Ridge Road, Athens, OH 45701; (740) 592-4643.

Overwintering Rosemary

Q: *I would like to overwinter my rosemary here in USDA Zone 5. How can I do it?*

A: Most varieties of this attractive woody herb are cold-hardy only to Zone 7 or 8, but the 'Arp' cultivar will overwinter in Zone 6 and sometimes in Zone 5 if you can keep the plant in a warm, sheltered location. 'Arp' was released by the U.S. National Arboretum after herb expert Madalene Hill discovered an 8-foot-wide, 40-year-old rosemary growing in Arp, Texas. Tests confirmed the plant to be hardy to –10° to –15°F.

While 'Arp' is cold-hardy, Madalene Hill recommends growing the young plants in pots that you bring indoors for the first two winters. Keep the potted plants in a sunny window of the coolest room you have. Water lightly, but keep the humidity high by setting the pots on a tray of pebbles and water. Mist the plants daily. (If white powdery mildew occurs, spray with Safer's sulfur-based fungicide.)

You can plant 2- or 3-year-old plants in the garden, but be sure the site has protection from prevailing winter winds as well as good drainage. Hill warns that rosemary is more likely to die from wind damaging its evergreen leaves than from cold killing its roots. 'Arp' is available from Goodwin Creek Gardens in Williams, Oregon (see "Resources" on page 234).

Tarragon in Oregon

Q: *Why can't I buy French tarragon seeds? Plants are expensive. Help!*

A: You can't buy the seed of French tarragon because such a thing does not exist! French tarragon, the type used in cooking, never sets viable seed. The only "tarragon" seed you *can* buy is Russian tarragon, which has little culinary value. With French tarragon, you *have* to start with a plant.

But you might not have to *buy* one. Perhaps you have a gardening friend with a big plant that's ready for springtime dividing. Tarragon easily survives those mild, Northwest winters west of the Cascades, and a small root division can grow into a large plant in just a couple of years. "The biggest problems you encounter growing tarragon in the Northwest are poor drainage and too much water in wintertime. But you can alleviate that by growing it in raised beds that contain lots of organic matter," assures Jim Becker of Goodwin Creek Gardens in Williams, Oregon.

SPICES & NUTS
Saffron Sources

Q: *Can you help us find a source so we can grow our own saffron?*

A: Saffron, one of the most expensive spices in the world, is harvested from an autumn-blooming crocus (*Crocus sativus*) that has been cultivated for at least 3,000 years for the unique, rich flavor of the thin stigmas in the center of each flower. Just ¼ ounce of dried saffron powder costs more than $40. Saffron crocus bulbs are not commonly offered by garden centers (probably because they need to be planted earlier in the autumn than most other flower bulbs), but you can order them from Bundles of Bulbs in Baltimore, Maryland (see "Resources" on page 234). The bulbs are shipped in August so that you can plant them immediately. That way, they'll begin blooming in October—and you'll have a wonderful display of fall color to enjoy.

Saffron crocus needs well-drained, sandy, alkaline soil and is hardy in USDA Zones 5 to 8. Heirloom-plant expert William Woys Weaver says the showy lavender flowers are magnificent in October and release a strong honey scent. Because the bulbs are dormant during the summer, Weaver suggests growing them with a mulch of shallow-rooted flowering annuals, such as moss rose (portulaca) so you don't end up with bare spots in your garden.

Dry your saffron harvest simply by spreading the stigmas on a plate. Each saffron flower has just three thin stigmas, so even though it takes only 1 inch of the potent spice to flavor one dish, you'll still need a good number of plants to produce enough saffron to use in cooking. Weaver estimates that it takes the dried threads from 50 to 100 bulbs to produce ⅛ of a teaspoon of saffron powder for a typical recipe.

Tree of Spice

Q: *While living in Latin America, I ate many foods seasoned with a paprika-like powder called achiote. Last year I found the spice in a local grocery store in a seed form called annatto. It was next to impossible to pulverize the seeds, so this year I stuck the remainder of them in some soil and they sprouted. How should I take care of the plants? And how do I grind the seeds?*

A: Give the young plant lots of light (a key factor), lots of water, and lots of space, and they will quickly grow into small flowering trees, explains David Bar-Zvi, Ph.D., curator of flowering ornamentals at the Fairchild Tropical Garden in Coral Gables, Florida. Native to South America, these little tropical trees are damaged by temperatures below 35°F. Since you appear to be located on the Gulf side of northern Florida, you probably experience freezing temperatures every winter, so you'll need to transplant your trees into movable pots that you can bring indoors during cold snaps. (Growing them in pots will also keep these trees much smaller than their natural 20-foot height.)

Grown outdoors in tropical areas, annatto (*Bixa orellana*) makes a good hedge and bee plant, adds Monica Moran Brandies, author of *Herbs and Spices for Florida Gardens* (B. B. Mackey Books, 1996). Annatto trees flower in the summer, producing pretty pink or white blooms that resemble wild roses, and attractive red or green seedpods. Fertilize annatto trees at the beginning of the growing season with any balanced organic fertilizer, but don't overfeed them or they won't produce many seeds, cautions Dr. Bar-Zvi.

The seed pods are mature when they stop growing. Open the pods, scrape out the orange seeds, and lay them on paper to dry. Handle carefully because the seedpod innards can leave stains. Good news: You don't have to grind the seeds to use them! "Take a cup or so of the seeds, heat them in a quart of oil, cool it, bottle it, and just use a tablespoon of that when you're cooking," says Dr. Bar-Zvi. "Annatto adds subtle flavorings to foods, but its value is more as a dye. In our region it's used to make rice yellow (much like saffron). It is also the dye from which the coloring for margarine is derived," he notes.

All about Pistachios

Q: *Can you tell me how to grow, harvest, and/or prepare pistachios?*

A: Pistachios (*Pistachia vera*) need long, hot, dry summers and moderately cold winters with no hard freezes. You'll need to plant one male tree to pollinate each seven or eight female trees in your grove, says Louise Ferguson, Ph.D., extension pomologist at the University of California's Kearney Agricultural Center. Plant your trees about 30 feet apart—they spread, and when properly pruned, older trees will be wider than they are tall. And they can get old—living for 1,000 years or so.

Grafted (budded) trees will begin to give you pistachios in about 5 years. Plant after all danger of frost has passed, but while the tree is still dormant. Pistachios, like other nut trees, have long central taproots, so you have to handle them carefully. As you add soil to the planting hole, water occasionally to settle the soil around the roots. At the surface, form a 6-inch-deep basin about 3 feet across around the tree. Fill it with water, don't water again until you see leaves begin to grow, and then fill the basin up about once per week (overwatering can cause fungus problems).

Each year before new growth begins, prune the tree into a vase shape: You want all the branches to point up. If any point up at less than a 45-degree angle, cut them off at the branch collar close to the trunk. Your nuts are ready to harvest when 8 out of 10 outer hulls pop off and the inside shell splits open when you squeeze the whole thing gently. Lay a sheet or tarp on the ground, and jostle the nut clusters with a pole to knock them down.

To dehull, put the nuts in a burlap bag, and bang the bag against a wall or hit it with a board. Dump the contents into a bucket of water; the hulls and empty nuts will float and the good meaty nuts will sink to the bottom. Lay the sinkers in the sun for a few days to dry, or freeze them right away and dry them in small batches as needed. If you like your plants with salt, you can swirl your nuts in salt water, drain, and dry them in a 350°F oven for a half hour.

Hulling Walnuts the Easy Way

Q: *My black-walnut tree produced 10 bushels of nuts this year. Is there an easy way to hull them?*

A: You can try a couple of methods. If you want to get some exercise while hulling, you could spread the black walnuts on a hard surface and walk all over them (wearing old shoes) to tread off their green, spongy covering.

If 10 bushels of walnuts is too many to dance on, however, spread them in the tire tracks of a gravel driveway and drive over them with your car. That's what Missouri folks with just one or two walnut trees do, says John Rickman, director of procurement for Hammons Products Company, a commercial sheller of eastern black walnuts, located in Stockton, Missouri. (Hammons does not drive over its walnuts to remove the hulls—the company uses commercial dehulling machines.) After the hulls are smashed, pick up the hard-shelled walnuts, and put them in a tub of water to float off the bad nuts. Also, be sure to wear thick rubber gloves when handling these nuts—the juice from their hulls leaves a dark stain on everything it touches.

Chapter

5

SEED STARTING & SAVING

Starting plants from seeds, saving seeds from your garden, and propagating plants can be fun and rewarding as well as a great way to share some of your favorites with family and friends. In this chapter, you'll find advice on everything from turning a pinecone into a pine tree to rooting roses successfully.

STARTING FROM SEED

Are Grow Lights Worthwhile?

Q: *Do those expensive grow lights advertised in garden catalogs really produce better seedlings than standard fluorescent tubes?*

A: No. According to the research we've reviewed, those special grow lights are not worth the extra expense. You can grow perfectly good seedlings beneath inexpensive fluorescent lights, which cost only $1 or $2 per 48-inch tube. Shop-light fixtures with two fluorescent tubes sell for as little as $10 at hardware stores and home centers.

When growing seedlings, leave the lights on for about 16 hours per day, and adjust your seedlings as they grow to keep them as close as possible to the lights without letting any leaves actually touch the tubes.

(Never try to grow plants using only regular incandescent lightbulbs—they don't provide the right spectrum of light, and they produce too much heat.)

Leggy Seedlings

Q: *Why do all my seedlings grow so tall and spindly in the greenhouse that they topple over before they develop their first true leaves?*

A: Plants with long, often weak stems may be suffering from any one of the following conditions: insufficient light, excessively high temperature, and crowding of plants.

Although you can't reshape a spindly seedling into a stocky, well-grown plant, you can take several steps to promote more normal growth from that point onward. Lower the temperature, thin plants, and, if possible, transplant the seedlings (transplant shock may slow their growth a bit). If you transplant the plants, make sure to set them deeper in their new containers.

To supply more light to plants, first be sure no trees, woodpiles, or other obstructions shade the greenhouse. Next, paint all interior walls and shelves with an exterior-grade, durable white paint to reflect more light on plants. Don't pile up bags of potting soil, clay pots, and other greenhouse supplies so that they cover parts of the white walls.

Harden Off Seedlings with a Coldframe

Q: *How do I use a coldframe to harden off seedlings? How long does it take?*

A: Using a coldframe to harden off seedlings is simple if you follow these guidelines from Eileen Weinsteiger, head gardener at the Rodale Institute Experimental Farm in Maxatawny, Pennsylvania.

"Most of the time, you have to keep the coldframe open so the seedlings get good ventilation," she says. "If you keep it closed, you could scorch them." Also, keep the seedlings moist, but don't overwater them—be especially careful about letting in too much rain.

"For early crops such as brassicas, put the seedlings in the coldframe 2 to 3 weeks before it's time to plant them in the garden," Weinsteiger says. Allow at least 2 weeks in the coldframe to harden off flowers and warm-season plants, such as tomatoes and peppers.

Keep the coldframe cover wide open during the day unless temperatures fall below 50°F, or if it rains hard. When daytime temperatures are below 50°F, just open the lid a little bit (¼ to 1 inch). Be sure to close the cover at night. "But if temperatures aren't going to drop below 50°F at night, you can keep the coldframe open," she says. If nighttime temperatures are forecasted to dip close to freezing, "you can put a rug on top of the frame for added insulation," Weinsteiger says.

Remember that internal coldframe temperatures can climb above 80°F—that's into the danger zone—on a 50°F day. Weinsteiger suggests putting a thermometer inside the coldframe to monitor the temperature.

Hot Peppers Need Heat, Too

Q: I've had great success in my hot pepper patch with the more common varieties, but when it comes to germinating exotics (habanero, piquin, chiltepin, or chimayo), I've had no luck at all. My flats are bottom-heated; the seed is fresh; I'm using starting soil is as recommended; sunlight, moisture, and nutrient levels are controlled; my attitude is good; and I talk to them. Que pasa?

A: "It's easy to have trouble growing hot peppers outside of the tropics and subtropics—they just haven't become adapted to temperate climates," says Craig Dremann of Redwood City Seed Company in Redwood City, California. For best germination, they need to be kept really warm—

daytime temperatures of about 85°F and night temperatures no less than 60° or 70°F. (Bell-type peppers have adapted to sprouting in cooler temperatures, he explains.)

Try putting the seed flat in an oven with its light on (but the oven itself off). Cover the flat with a piece of plastic wrap to keep moisture in. As soon as the plants sprout, take them out of the oven, remove the plastic, and water them.

If warm temperatures fail to sprout your seeds, you have another, less-organic option, Dremann says. Chiltepins and piquins are called "bird peppers" because they are a favorite food of these creatures. To simulate being eaten by birds (the natural "wake-up call" that tells a wild pepper seed it's time to start growing), he soaks his seeds in a solution of ½ teaspoon of saltpeter to 1 quart of water for 4 hours before planting. The nitrogen in the saltpeter (14 percent) simulates the contents of a bird's digestive track, Dremann says.

However, some organic certification groups prohibit the use of saltpeter (potassium nitrate, or KNO_3) because its nitrogen is highly soluble and because most is factory-produced by chemical reaction. Mined saltpeter does exist but is difficult to come by.

Could you get the same result by soaking the seeds in a strong solution of a high-nitrogen organic fertilizer? Organic sources that come close to saltpeter's concentration include bloodmeal, bat guano, and fish meal. Fungus problems could occur with these sources, so rinse your seeds after soaking.

Daisies vs. Impatiens

Q: *I planted seeds of gloriosa daisies and impatiens at the same time and treated them the same way. Both trays of seeds were exposed to light and were heated by a warm radiator. The daisies emerged in* *less than 2 weeks and the impatiens, except for four recent (and paltry) seedlings, were a great disappointment. What went wrong?*

A: You probably buried both kinds of seeds deep in your seed-starting mix. Impatiens are one of the many flowers whose seeds need to be *exposed* to light to germinate. If you want to cover impatiens seed to keep the seed reliably moist, you should only do so with a *very* light touch of *very* fine vermiculite. (Daisies sprout quite nicely when covered deeply.) Simon Crawford, technical specialist at PanAmerican Seeds (the behemoth of seed wholesalers), says that the next time you try to sprout impatiens seeds, *don't* bury them, but *do* mist the sowing medium lightly several times a day, if possible. Keeping the moisture at a nice damp level is especially crucial when the seeds crack open, says Crawford.

Hasta la Hosta

Q: *Can you tell me how to grow hostas from seed?*

A: It's actually a good idea to start your own hostas from seed—these shade-loving ornamentals readily cross-pollinate, so you can expect to get some interesting new varieties when you grow your own this way. You might even get something as unique as the unusual-looking 'On Stage,' which has gold leaves with dark green margins and is also unusually expensive—it can set you back $75 *per plant!*

What's more, growing hostas from seed is *very easy*, says Mary Ann Metz, greenhouse manager for Klehm Nursery in Champaign, Illinois. Fill a container with a soil-less seed-starting mix, moisten it, place the seeds on top, and cover them thinly with about ¼ inch of the seed-starting mix, depending on the size of the seeds. You can use potting soil instead (it often contains the same stuff as seed-starting mixes), says Metz, but don't use regular garden soil.

Keep your seed-starting medium moist but not soggy and somewhere around room temperature, and in a couple weeks you should have baby hostas. "You can plant them outside as soon as they are big enough to handle and have good root systems," says Metz. Mulch them well their first winter, just as you would any new plant, she adds.

You might want to grow these self-sown hostas in a "holding area" of some kind until you can tell just how tall they're going to get—they could well be anywhere from a couple inches to a couple feet high. Move them to a permanent home in your landscape after they achieve their final height. Note in choosing the final spot that hostas with light centers can take less sun than ones with yellow, blue, or dark green leaves.

Seeds to Trees

Q: *How do you start peach, plum, and apricot trees from seed?*

A: You can grow these trees by planting their fruit pits, but chances are, the fruit they'll bear won't be as good as that of the original tree. Fruit from seed-grown trees is often small and green, says Richard Funt, Ph.D., director of the consumer horticulture center at Ohio State University.

The best way to get good, productive fruit trees is to go to a knowledgeable nursery and buy grafted trees. These are trees that combine rootstocks that are disease- and pest-resistant and scions (or fruiting branches) of varieties that will bear superior fruit.

You can still use your fruit pits to grow rootstock for your own grafting attempts. Here are the basics:

Clean the pits, and dry and store them in a cool area with low humidity where they won't become moldy or dry out. When soil temperatures fall to about 40°F, plant the pits about 6 inches apart and 2 inches deep in good, well-drained soil. The pits need about 120 days of temperatures below 40°F before they'll sprout; expect about a 50 percent germination rate.

To protect them from rodent damage, cover the pits with the first inch of soil, then put down wire mesh, and cover that with the second inch, advises Dr. Funt. Remove the mesh about April 1, before the seeds begin to sprout. Water the seedlings well, but don't fertilize them too much. Let them grow through one complete season, then graft the kind of fruit you want onto them.

Turning a Pinecone into a Pine Tree

Q: *How do I plant a pinecone to start a new seedling?*

A: You don't—a pinecone is really a kind of giant seed packet that contains lots of individual pine-tree seeds. The seeds trapped in the cone are what you want to plant. To get to those seeds, pick the cone just as it turns from green to brown—generally late summer or fall—and dry it; the scales will pop open and seeds will fall out, says John Kuser, Ph.D., associate professor at Rutgers University's department of natural resources in New Brunswick, New Jersey.

For successful germination, however, some pine seeds require "cold stratification," which entails subjecting them to a simulated winter. To achieve this illusion, soak the seeds in a glass of water overnight to get them to swell up, then drain and place them in a little plastic bag in the refrigerator for a month. Time this endeavor so that they come out of the fridge around March, then plant the seeds about ¼ inch deep in little pots on your windowsill. Water thoroughly, and cover with a piece of clear plastic to retain moisture.

When the seed sprouts (in 10 days to 3 weeks), remove the plastic. Dr. Kuser says he's grown loblolly, white, pitch, shortleaf, and Virginia pines this way. Pitch-pine cones need to be heated to get them to open up. In this case, you're simulating the heat of a forest fire, which sets off the pitch-pines reproduction cycle in the wild. Dip the cones in boiling water for 5 seconds, then dry for a week in a warm, sunny spot. (If they don't open, repeat and increase the hot dip to 10 seconds.)

When your pines are about 3 inches high, plant them outdoors in a protected spot, and keep them well watered and well weeded for the first season. If you want to keep your seedlings in containers until they are big enough to survive on their own, be sure they get lots of water and full sun. The only pine that doesn't need a lot of sun, says Dr. Kuser, is the white pine, which can take partial shade.

SAVING SEEDS
Don't Heat the Beans

Q: *I've read what appears to be conflicting information about beans. Now I don't know whether or not to save beans for next year's seed, and if so, whether or not to heat the seeds in an oven immediately after harvest to kill any internal critters.*

A: Sure, you can save bean seeds for next year's garden, but you shouldn't heat them. "Temperatures warmer than 95°F will damage the seeds. Heat beans only if you are

going to store them for eating. If you intend to plant them, freezing them is a much better pest-control technique," says Kent Whealy, director of the Seed Savers Exchange in Decorah, Iowa.

To freeze properly, air-dry the seeds until a test bean shatters instead of mashes when hit with a hammer on a hard surface. (If they aren't dry enough, freezing will damage them.) Then put them in a freezer for 2 days to kill any bean weevil eggs beneath the seed coats. (Weevils are the critters that hatch and bore little round holes into stored beans.) Store your beans in a cool, dry place until planting time arrives next year. (Big exception: If your beans have green or yellow patterns on the leaves—symptoms of mosaic viruses—don't save them for seed. Find a new, uncontaminated supply instead.)

Breeding Peppers

Q: *How can I improve an heirloom pepper variety?*

A: Save seeds from the best fruits of plants having traits you wish to encourage, says Larry Lansdowne, seed germinator for Seeds Blum, a seed company based in Boise, Idaho, that specializes in heirloom varieties. Consider traits such as plant size, fruit size, number of fruits, insect resistance, earliness, and, of course, flavor.

Cull poor plants early, before they flower. "Hand-pollinate selected flowers and cover them with a paper or plastic bag," says Chris Wien, associate professor of vegetable crops at Cornell University in Ithaca, New York. "Otherwise, as much as 20 percent of peppers will cross-pollinate, usually due to bee activity." For highest germination next season, obtain seeds from fully ripe peppers.

Before harvesting seeds, store mature peppers for 1 month in a dry area indoors, then label and refrigerate seeds in an airtight container and include a desiccant. Maintain adequate records of your trials, especially growing conditions, cultural practices, plant characteristics, and details of harvesting, seed cleaning, and seed storage. Be patient and flexible—don't expect immediate results, says Lansdowne. Even with the best conditions, yields can vary for unexplained reasons. It may be years before you see some of the improvement you desire.

The Potato of My Eye

Q: *For the past two years, I've cut the eyes from potatoes in fall and stored them for spring planting. Even though they're spread out in a single layer in shallow cardboard boxes, they either dry up or get moldy. What am I doing wrong?*

A: You should try to store the whole potato and not just the eyes, says Dave Ronniger of Ronniger's Seed Potatoes in Moyie Springs, Idaho. "By removing the eye from the potato, you expose the eye's fleshy parts to bacteria and mold," he says.

To prevent your seed potatoes from drying out, store them in mesh bags, boxes, or bins in a root cellar or basement where humidity is high (around 80 to 90 percent) and the temperature is between 36° and 40°F. Or try storing them underground in a pit, covered with dirt, sand, or mulch, or in a box in an unheated garage.

Wherever you store them, don't pile them too deep; this cuts down on air circulation and could bruise the spuds on the bottom of the pile.

CHECK IT OUT!

Preserve the germination power of your leftover seeds by storing them in your refrigerator. Researchers at Kansas State University say keeping your seeds refrigerated will help them last up to 10 times longer than seeds stored at room temperature. Store your seeds in an airtight, moisture-proof container (like a glass jar) along with a small amount of moisture-absorbing silica gel (available at craft stores). And never leave the packets sitting around open. An hour of exposure on a humid day can reduce storage life by half!

'Brandywines' Forever

Q: *I'm growing 'Brandywine' tomatoes this year for the first time. Can I save the seeds from this year's crop for planting again next year, or do I have to buy new seeds?*

A: 'Brandywine' tomatoes are open-pollinated, so yes, you can save the seeds, plant them next year, and get 'Brandywines' again, says Russ Waldrop, co-owner of Santa Barbara Heirloom Seedling Nursery in Santa Barbara, California. 'Brandywine', one of the most famous heirloom varieties, is believed to have originated in Chester County, Pennsylvania, in the late 1800s—and you are about to become part of its long and storied tradition. After all, the only reason that heirlooms like 'Brandywine' are around today is that *generations* of gardeners have saved their seeds—just as you now intend to do.

But you can't just "save" tomato seeds like those of peppers or pumpkins; there's a specific process that must be followed. In *Seed to Seed,* a very detailed book on seed saving (Seed Saver Publications, 1991), the author Suzanne Ashworth explains: To get rid of the sticky, gelatinous coating that surrounds the seeds, float the seeds in an open jar of water and set the jar aside. The mix will start to ferment. After 3 days, add more water, cover the jar and shake it up. The 'viable' tomato seeds (the ones that will reliably sprout for you next year) will sink and the bad ones (and other gunk) will float. Skin off that top stuff, strain out the good seeds, spread them out to dry in a cool, dim, airy spot, and then keep them in a closed jar in a cool, dry place. If you have any silica gel—those little moisture-absorbing packets that come with vitamins and shoes and say "don't eat"—place one or two of them in the jar with your seeds.

Can I Save Seedless Watermelon Seeds?

Q: *Can I produce seeds to propagate my own crop of seedless watermelon? If I plant the seeds I have saved from an overripe 'Jack of Hearts' seedless watermelon, will I get seedless melons next year?*

A: Unfortunately, producing seed for seedless watermelon is difficult, time-consuming, labor-intensive, and expensive. Seed crops fail almost as often as they succeed, says Gary Nepa, product manager for Petoseed Company (creators of the 'Jack of Hearts' variety), and the seed you have saved probably will not even produce a plant next year.

And that's because what you've saved probably is not really a seed. Nepa says that when a seedless melon overmatures, it produces what looks like seed, but they usually are just seed coats that don't contain any endosperm. Producing your own seedless watermelon seed is nearly impossible because these melons are the result of unique genetic combinations that must be performed for each batch of seed.

Seedless melons have three sets of chromosomes (and are called triploids). Regular melons have two sets (diploids). To create a seedless melon, a regular one is crossed with a tetraploid, a melon that's been treated with substances similar to growth hormones so that it has four sets of chromosomes. This cross produces the seedless watermelon you know and love.

Chapter

6

COMPOST & SOIL

All great gardens start with the same basic ingredient: healthy soil. You can achieve healthy soil by working in compost and adding the right organic fertilizer. In this chapter, you'll find information to help you on that quest for great soil, such as what not to throw in your compost pile and why crop rotation is important.

COMPOST & SOIL

COMPOSTING CONUNDRUMS

Compost du Jour

Q: *I've accumulated grass clippings from a very large yard, manure from several steer, a few bags of leaves, and spent plants from my garden. Can you suggest a compost recipe for these ingredients? How should I store the compost this fall and winter until I can use it next spring?*

A: Cary Oshins, composting specialist at the Rodale Institute Experimental Farm in Maxatawny, Pennsylvania, says that a mix of 1 part grass clippings, 1 part garden residues, 3 parts leaves, and 2 parts manure (which he assumes is mixed with bedding material like straw) should give you a fairly good ratio of carbon to nitrogen, the key to successful composting.

By mixing the ingredients well to begin with, you can save yourself some turning later, he adds. And if you have access to finished compost, "cover the pile with some immediately after you're finished mixing up the raw ingredients," he advises. "Then when the pile begins to cool and the outside starts to look dry, mix the outside edges into the center so that those parts get composted as well. In 2 months, it should be finished."

Few people worry about storing their compost over the winter. If you're *sure* it's finished composting, you can cover it with a tarp or something else that's waterproof to keep rain and snow from leaching out any of the nutrients. But be *sure* it is finished—that is, finely decomposed and sweet smelling. If you throw a tarp over unfinished compost, it will block air flow and delay decomposition. If in doubt, just let it sit out.

Dog Doo Is a Don't

Q: *I live with two vegetarian dogs. Can I recycle their manure by composting it?*

A: "Vegetarian dogs do not have a lower incidence of parasites," explains Michael W. Fox, D.V.M., nationally known veterinarian and vice president of the Humane Society of the United States. Dogs pick up parasites very easily from other dogs (via all that licking and rolling around), and the only reliable way to know if your dogs have parasites is to take a stool sample to your vet's office for testing. You *can't* tell just by checking droppings for visible signs of worms, says Dr. Fox, because worms aren't always excreted.

And if your hounds *are* infected with roundworms, their microscopic eggs could easily survive their time in the compost pile, especially if it's not a *very* hot pile, adds Dr. Fox. Plus, if you then put compost-containing roundworm eggs into your vegetable garden, the eggs could easily hitch a ride on salad or root crops, and hatch in your intestinal tract. From there they may migrate to other parts of the body, including the eyes, where they can cause blindness.

A *very* active composting process (170°F for 3 days) is enough to destroy roundworm eggs, says Ann Rippy, a conservation agronomist with the Fairbanks Soil and Water Conservation District in Alaska. But her information comes from observation of a very detailed and exacting formal program ongoing up there. Composting dog waste is a hot issue in Alaska because of pollution from the manure of the many sled dogs used for winter transportation. Composting experiments have been underway there for years, trying to reduce the risks of parasite passage. Unless you're a certified master with a guaranteed super-hot pile, don't depend on your home compost pile to reach the degree of heat necessary here.

Sick Compost?

Q: *Can I add "sick" material—such as diseased tomato vines or blighted peony flowers—to my compost pile? What about seed-laden debris from noxious weeds?*

A: Depends on how hot your pile gets as it composts. If you pile your compost in large heaps and turn it frequently, you'll usually destroy pathogens and weed seeds. But if you're a lazy composter, you've probably got a cold pile, and you shouldn't throw "sick" stuff in.

"If the internal pile temperature exceeds 113°F for a long time period or 140°F for a short time, most disease-causing pathogens die," says Harry A. J. Hoitink, Ph.D., compost expert and plant pathologist at Ohio State University.

There are exceptions, he explains, but for the most part, heat kills diseases. Even in the cooler parts of the pile (68° to 95°F), many pathogens will be killed by the microbial activity going on in the compost pile itself. The pathogens are either parasitized by the good microbes or die of starvation from competing with good microbes for food, Dr. Hoitink says.

But to destroy most weed seeds, compost must reach high temperatures (140° to 160°F) on the inside of the pile for at least 3 days. Since certain parts of the pile may not achieve such high temperatures, mixing in seed-laden weed material can be very risky.

Whether or not to add weeds or diseased plants to your compost pile is a matter of degree (just how diseased are the plants?) and proportion (how much do you intend to put on the pile?), says Cyane Gresham, compost researcher at the Rodale Institute Experimental Farm in Maxatawny, Pennsylvania. If plants are heavily infested or if the disease in question has been a persistent problem in your garden, keep that plant out of the pile. It's just not worth the risk, she says.

Don't build a pile heavily laden with sick plants or weeds either—such stuff should only make up a small proportion of the mix. And remember that compost doesn't heat up in late fall and winter as much as it does in the summer months.

Potential Poisons

Q: *I read a lot about gardeners traveling up, down, and around to roadsides, neighbors' yards, and landfills to gather clippings and brush to compost for their gardens. What if these sources have been sprayed or dusted with insecticides and herbicides?*

Q: *I'm a floral designer and for years I've used flower-shop waste in my compost pile, along with grass clippings and kitchen and garden wastes. Am I poisoning my compost and my garden with insecticide residues by doing this?*

Q: *I have access to an unlimited supply of grass clippings from a local golf course. I know they are sprayed with herbicides. Can I put them directly on my garden? If not, how long should I wait before using the clippings?*

A: All good questions. Unfortunately, there are no easy answers. According to the University of Illinois Center for Solid Waste Management Research, some common herbicides can stay active for a full year.

"Once these herbicides are introduced into your garden, some could be taken up by plants. So, yes—theoretically, you may get traces of these toxins in the food you grow," says Joe Pignatello, Ph.D., a scientist who studies pesticide breakdown at the Connecticut Agricultural Experiment Station.

Scientific research on how pesticides and herbicides break down in the compost pile is just beginning, but the consensus is that some of these substances may survive the composting process. Whether they do or not depends on just which pesticide or herbicide was used; different chemicals break down at different rates. And the conditions within the compost pile (heat, moisture, pH, etc.) also affect the rate at which they disappear.

With all these variables, there's just no way for the average backyard gardener to tell when (or if) compost ingredients that started out tainted become safe for organic food growing. So, the answer for the truly organic is no—just don't do it. Don't use herbicide- or pesticide-treated plant material as mulch, and don't add it to your compost pile.

In case this warning comes too late, and you already have some golf-course trimmings and who knows what kind of questionable clippings in your heap, don't despair. You can speed up the breakdown process and get rid of toxic residues as fast as possible (and more completely) by tuning up your compost pile itself.

"Herbicide and insecticide molecules are more readily degraded under aerobic conditions," says Olli H. Tuovinen, Ph.D., professor of microbiology at Ohio State University. And the best way to achieve those conditions is to turn your pile frequently. The more often you turn your compost, the more air you add, and the faster the pesticides will break down.

And don't neglect your pile's carbon-to-nitrogen ratio. "If there is too much carbon, the pH is lowered and microbial activity will be inhibited," thus slowing the breakdown process, says Dr. Tuovinen. If you're using a lot of leaves or other high-carbon materials, add a nitrogen source—

preferably a nice hot one like fresh manure or crushed-up shellfish shells—to your pile.

Always add some garden soil, too. The microflora in soil are crucial to the composting process, explains Dr. Tuovinen.

Dry Pile Problems

Q: *I have a hard time keeping my compost pile moist here in Arizona. I've been covering it loosely with black plastic to reduce evaporation, but I'm not sure whether I'm doing more harm than good. What's your advice?*

A: Loosely covering compost piles is a good idea in both very dry and very rainy climates. The materials will decompose fastest if you can keep them constantly moist; but never let them get waterlogged. Covering your pile might reduce the flow of oxygen slightly, but not enough to offset the benefits. "Layers of coarse stems and brush sometimes let too much air into the pile, causing it to dry out even in less arid climes than Arizona," says Cyane Gresham, compost researcher at the Rodale Institute Experimental Farm in Maxatawny, Pennsylvania. If you're using coarse material, Gresham suggests that you cut it up before adding it to the pile; then cover the coarse layer with some soil to help hold moisture.

Teeming Compost Tumbler

Q: *My compost tumbler is teeming with maggots, even though I've sealed up the holes with duct tape and plastic. How can I kill the maggots without wrecking the compost?*

A: Compost that's too wet, anaerobic, and putrid (the result of too much green material) could become a haven for maggots, says Cary Oshins, composting specialist with the

Rodale Institute Experimental Farm in Maxatawny, Pennsylvania. "If so, I'd mix in some sawdust and some finished compost to dry things down and favor the microbes over the macrofauna."

"Maggots should not be a problem in a good, working compost pile that is heating up and being turned regularly," adds Nancy Roe, Ph.D., extension horticulturist with Texas A&M Extension Service. An optimal ratio of one-third kitchen and garden wastes to two-thirds dead, brown stuff, plus a shovelful of finished compost will decompose quickly, becoming hot enough to kill maggots. After the materials heat up, you can begin turning the pile, advises Dr. Roe.

When you add kitchen scraps, cover them with a handful of brown material to keep the flies from laying their eggs on them. Also, avoid putting meat in your compost tumbler. "Most of the time when I get a call about maggots, it's because someone has put meat or fish scraps in the bin," says Spring Gillard, compost hot-line operator/educator for City Farmer's compost demonstration garden and hot line in Vancouver, British Columbia.

You must also unseal your tumbler. Those holes you taped shut are there for a reason. To decompose properly, the organic materials inside need air.

Rats Be Gone

Q: *We've had a recurring problem with rats getting into our compost pile. What can we do?*

A: Contrary to classic advice about compost, city dwellers such as yourself might have to keep vegetable food wastes out of your pile. Madelon Bolling, compost hot-line operator for Seattle Tilth, says rodents are attracted to fruit and vegetable scraps—cucumber peels, melon rinds, citrus, etc.—in a pile. (Of course, you should never put dairy, meat, fat, or oil-type wastes in your compost—these will attract animals anywhere; and they slow decomposition.)

Some basic advice for composters with rat problems:

- Keep your compost pile hot enough (140° to 170°F) to decompose vegetable scraps quickly. Chop wastes fine, turn the pile frequently, and combine materials that will give you a 25:1 carbon-to-nitrogen ratio.

- Use a rodent-resistant composter such as a tumbler. Rodent-proof composters need to be made of metal, with no opening larger than ½ inch. (Or enclose all sides of an existing nonmetal structure in hardware cloth or screen with openings of ½ inch or less.) Mix your vegetable scraps with yard waste, and keep them in the center of the pile.

- Limit your compost pile to inedible plant materials such as leaves, weeds, grass clippings, twigs, wood chips, and so forth, and get a worm box for your garbage.

- Clean up any fallen fruits, vegetables, pet feces, and so forth, that might initially attract the pests to the area around your pile.

- Keep your compost pile moist—this will keep rats from nesting in it during cold or wet seasons.

- Check for improperly managed garbage—which is the main cause of rodent problems—in your area. Is there a restaurant nearby with outside trash cans? Is your municipality contributing to the problem by stockpiling garbage where rats can get into it? Are your neighbors messy? Rats are usually a community-wide problem, not a one-household occurrence.

Lastly, a Canadian group has published "Urban Home Composting: Rodent-Resistant Bins and Environmental Health Standards," a 36-page pamphlet that includes plans for building pest-proof compost bins. Contact City Farmer, 801-318 Homer Street, Vancouver, BC, Canada V6B 2V3, or visit their Web site www.cityfarmer.org.

Composting in the Trenches

Q: *What are the advantages of trench composting, and how do I do it?*

A: For rapid improvement of poor soils, you can't beat trench composting. It's like an underground mulch, ideal for wastes that may be too obnoxious to have lying around on the surface of the ground, and for wastes (especially food scraps) that attract critters, says Cyane Gresham, compost researcher at the Rodale Institute Experimental Farm in Maxatawny, Pennsylvania. This method is especially advantageous in arid regions where aboveground piles typically dry out too fast; it helps retain the moisture the compost needs to break down.

Trench composting works best with small amounts of high-nitrogen materials such as grass clippings and food scraps. Don't bury too much stuff that won't break down quickly. Also, trench compost does not heat up the way a pile does, so don't bury disease-ridden plants or seed-laden weeds.

Ready to try it? Dig your trench about 12 inches deep and 18 inches wide (and as long as you want), pack it with your raw materials, wet it down, and cover with soil. Allow the compost a season to decompose and then just plant a garden bed right on top of it.

Caution: Uncured Compost

Q: *Our town has a composting program that uses collected yard waste. The first couple of seasons that our community composters tried making compost, they got poor results (and terrible odors!). But after those false starts, the program seemed to be working. So last spring I added about 6 inches of it to half my raised vegetable beds. What a big mistake. It reduced yields by two-thirds. My caged tomatoes that used to be 5-foot-high plants loaded with fruit only reached 2 feet in height—and had very few tomatoes. Climbing green beans grew only 2 feet tall and produced no beans. Peppers, okra, and cucumbers were all stunted. Where I didn't apply the town compost, I had my normal, good yields. What went wrong, and what do I do now?*

A: What did that town compost look and smell like when you added it to your garden? It should have been dark brown and crumbly with an earthy smell. If it was still hot, or if you could still see uncomposted twigs and leaves, it may have been unfinished. And compost that isn't sufficiently broken down when you apply it can tie up nutrients as it continues to decompose in your garden, warns Steve Rioch, soil consultant at Timberleaf Farms in Albany, Ohio.

Rioch is also concerned about using smelly compost. "A bad smell indicates that the compost decomposed anaerobically [without getting enough oxygen]. This lack of oxygen could create compounds that can be toxic to plants," he explains. If the officials can't seem to get it right and you still want to make use of this resource, consider aerating some "town compost" yourself, he suggests, by recomposting a batch until all of the original ingredients are unrecognizable and the pile has an earthy aroma.

If the problem was caused by incomplete decomposition, your existing compost will probably correct itself in the

Let your eyes and nose be your guide when trying to decide whether your compost is mature and ready for the garden. Finished compost should be loose and crumbly and you shouldn't be able to recognize the original ingredients you threw in the pile. Ideally, your compost should be slightly moist, but not soggy, and dark brown or almost black in color. Finally, take a sniff—if your compost smells like the good earth, you've struck "black gold."

garden as decomposition naturally continues. In any case, don't add any more town compost to your garden this year—that 6 inches last year should do you for a while. And the next time you help yourself to free compost, be *sure* it's finished by bringing it home and letting it "set a spell" before using it.

Work That Compost

Q: *How can I work compost into my rose garden and perennial flowerbeds without digging up and destroying the plants? Shouldn't compost be at the plants' root level to do the best job?*

A: You don't have to rip up your precious plants just to give them a little food. In fact, just mulching 2 to 4 inches of compost right on top of the soil in your flowerbeds will fight disease better than burying it at root level.

Don't worry about compost nutrients reaching your plants—that's what rain is for. Rain gradually leaches all the valuable stuff right down into the soil for you, and it's a bit more gentle to the flowers than your forcing the compost down to root level with a shovel.

Compost isn't just food for your flowers either—it can also protect plants from a variety of diseases. And you'll maximize the disease prevention just by applying compost to the surface of your beds, not burying it 6 feet under.

Timing? Eileen Weinsteiger, head gardener at the Rodale Institute Experimental Farm in Maxatawny, Pennsylvania, puts most of the compost on the farm's perennial beds in spring, side-dressing with some compost in summer and again in fall if plants need a boost. (Make sure to use only well-rotted compost; stuff that hasn't completely composted can burn plants.)

ADDING INGREDIENTS

Acid Lovers in Alkaline Soils

Q: *I'm very confused about organic soil treatments for growing acid-loving plants, such as camellias and gardenias, in my alkaline California soil. Can you help?*

A: Before you begin adding amendments to your soil, have your soil tested. That's the only way to know its exact pH and the probable reasons for its alkalinity, which will help determine your course of action.

The causes of alkalinity are many, but a high pH is not necessarily bad, states Stuart Pettygrove, Ph.D., cooperative extension soils specialist at the University of California at Davis. "It's not that some plants need acid soil, it's that they need some nutrient that is being tied up in the soil by an alkaline condition."

The most common remedy (but not necessarily the best, as we'll explain later) for alkaline soils is to add sulfur, which is converted by soil bacteria into sulfuric acid. Sulfuric acid lowers the soil's pH and makes certain nutrients more available. Sulfur products usually come with a label that tells you how many pounds to spread per 1,000 square feet, depending on your soil's initial pH and how much lower you want it to be. It should be spread and worked into the top 6 inches of soil. Usually between 4 and 8 pounds per 1,000 square feet are required. More is required if the soil contains a significant amount of lime (calcium carbonate). Also, soil containing lots of clay or calcium will require more sulfur than a sandy soil. A follow-up pH check could be helpful.

"You can easily overdo sulfur applications, so be conservative and let the process work slowly," Dr. Pettygrove

cautions. "It doesn't happen overnight. It can take weeks or months for the microbes to break down the sulfur."

Sulfur can also kill beneficial organisms in the soil and in most cases is not the most appropriate solution. If your soil is high in sodium or other soluble salts, you can balance the soil's pH by adding gypsum (calcium sulfate). This will have an acidifying effect and will flush out these salts, says John Farrell, garden manager at the Center for Agroecology and Sustainable Food Systems at the University of California at Santa Cruz.

A rough rule of thumb is to broadcast 4 to 6 pounds of gypsum per 100 square feet, then work it into the top 4 to 6 inches of the soil. "It's important to keep the soil moist," Farrell notes. A slower method of changing pH is to work an acid material such as peat moss, which has a pH of 3.5 to 4.5, into the root zone of individual plants while planting them, suggests Farrell. And don't overlook the benefits of organic matter. Use lots of straw, cover crops, and compost, which microorganisms will break down into mild organic acids.

Finally, you may be able to give plants the nutrients they aren't getting from the soil by spraying them directly onto the leaves. Frequent applications of kelp extract to the plant's leaves may be a good, subtle source of micronutrients that are commonly tied up under alkaline conditions, suggests Farrell.

For more specific advice, check with a garden-supply center or agricultural products company that is familiar with organic practices, such as Peaceful Valley Farm Supply in Grass Valley, California (see "Resources" on page 234). Peaceful Valley also offers a very complete soil testing service that includes recommendations that a staff person will be happy to discuss with you.

An Ash of a Different Color

Q: *Are ashes from a coal-burning stove or boiler safe to use in the vegetable garden?*

Q: *Would coal ashes be good for blueberry transplants? I have to drop my soil's pH level down 2 points.*

A: No. Coal ashes can contain lead, arsenic, and other undesirable elements. Children playing in the soil might ingest these unpleasantries, or plants might take them up, warns Dale E. Baker, Ph.D., professor of soil chemistry at Penn State University.

Right now, says Dr. Baker, the best way to dispose of coal ashes is to send them with other nonrecyclables to a landfill, or spread them on land that is not producing food.

Not all coal ash contains toxic substances, but testing to determine exactly what's in a certain supply of ash (or the coal itself) is expensive, he adds.

More Ash Advice

Q: *What about the black stuff I get from the chimney of my wood stove?*

A: "It has a very high pH and would be toxic to plants," says Peter Labosky, Ph.D., professor of wood science and technology at Penn State University. And this soot contains wood creosote, which is similar to coal tar creosote, a known carcinogen. All uses of coal tar creosote, except as a wood preservative, were revoked by the Environmental Protection Agency in 1984. Send it to a landfill or bury it far away from your edible plants.

Bones for Bulbs

Q: *I heard that because of a change in processing procedures, bonemeal has lost a great deal of its phosphate value and therefore its usefulness for fertilizing tulip and daffodil bulbs. I write a weekly garden column for our local newspaper, so I am interested in knowing the facts.*

A: Bonemeal is still an excellent organic source of phosphorus, although it may not be the best fertilizer to topdress your bulbs with. Joel Padmore, Ph.D., chairman of the Fertilizer Terms and Definitions Committee for the American Plant Food Control Officials, oversaw a laboratory analysis of 16 bonemeal products in response to a complaint in North Carolina and "found that most bonemeals were underguaranteed—there was more phosphorus than was listed on the labels." He also found that "most of the products contained around 6 percent nitrogen, even if the label didn't list nitrogen as a guaranteed ingredient."

How much nitrogen a bonemeal contains depends on how much meat is on the bones before they're ground up, which depends on the processor. In some cases, the nitrogen-rich materials are used for other purposes.

This distinction is important. Paul Nelson, Ph.D., professor of horticulture at North Carolina State University, says his bulb research shows that "most soils are not deficient in phosphorus, and the only major nutrient that is likely to be deficient is nitrogen." Bonemeal is still an excellent material to add to the soil below the bulbs when you first plant them to ensure they have a phosphorus reserve to draw on over the years. But phosphorus added to the soil surface after the bulbs are planted probably won't reach the roots, since phosphorus—unlike nitrogen and potassium—does not move very far in most soils.

Dr. Nelson recommends adding compost plus some bloodmeal or other high-nitrogen fertilizer to keep your bulbs in top shape. Each 100 square feet of bulbs needs at least 5 ounces of nitrogen for good root and leaf development. (If you have 100 ounces of fertilizer that's labeled 5 percent nitrogen, 5 of those ounces are nitrogen.)

And Dr. Nelson adds that you should apply fertilizer annually in the fall. "Unlike perennials, trees, and shrubs, which should not be fertilized in the fall, bulbs should be fed in October and November when their roots are actively growing."

Bonemeal and Mad Cows

Q: *I just finished reading* Deadly Feasts *by Richard Rhodes (Simon & Schuster, 1997), a book about mad cow disease. He investigated the connection between cannibalism, infected meat, and the use of garden bonemeal. Britain has already banned certain uses of bonemeal. Is it safe to use in the United States? What other products can a gardener use in its place?*

A: First, an explanation for other readers: Britain has a serious problem with mad cow disease, the common name for bovine spongiform encephalopathy (BSE), a disease that eats away brain tissue and causes loss of muscle coordination, seizures, and odd behavior. Since the epidemic came to light in 1986, hundreds of thousands of infected cattle have been destroyed in Britain. Scientists theorized that the outbreak was the result of the practice of feeding cows a protein food made from bonemeal and the waste body parts of animals infected with BSE or scrapie, a similar disease that affects sheep.

Humans have their own versions of these transmissible spongiform encephalopathies (TSEs). One, kuru, was traced to the practice of cannibalism in a New Guinea tribe. In

March 1996, the British government announced that the most likely explanation for 10 cases of a new variant of Creutzfeldt-Jacob disease, the human equivalent of mad cow disease, was exposure to BSE. Since then, the number of confirmed cases has doubled; no one knows how many more will occur because the incubation period of the disease can be 10 years long.

In December 1997, the British government banned the sale of most cuts of beef on the bone after researchers said there was a slight possibility that mad cow disease could be carried in beef bones and marrow. Even before that, however, the use of bovine-based products such as bonemeal had been banned from use as a fertilizer for commercial vegetable growing in Britain.

The situation in the United States is different. No cases of BSE have been reported here, and the United States does not import cattle, meat, or certain bovine-based products such as bone or bonemeal from countries where the disease occurs.

Still, BSE-free bonemeal is not 100 percent guaranteed. "We produce a lot of bonemeal domestically, but producers may be getting material from overseas. The disease has a long incubation period, and that means we might get material from a country that might report it in the future. While there are controls, and the risk might be lower in the United States than in other countries, the risk may not be zero," says Morris Potter, D.V.M., assistant director for foodborne diseases at the Centers for Disease Control and Prevention in Atlanta.

How to handle bonemeal? While we have no evidence that bonemeal poses a risk, Dr. Potter recommends wearing a mask and gloves and being careful when using this product. "One would also have to worry that one could inoculate oneself by getting stabbed by a rose thorn or a splinter that's covered with the stuff," he cautions.

Bonemeal is used as a plant food because of its high phosphorus content. If you want to forswear bonemeal, you could add phosphorus to your soil by boosting its organic matter content with compost and cover crops, such as legumes or buckwheat. You could also use rock phosphate or soft rock (colloidal) phosphate. (Wear a mask when handling colloidal phosphate because it's a very fine powder.) Fish emulsion or fish-based fertilizers also supply small amounts of phosphorus.

Fertile Grounds

Q: *I have a coffee machine going 12 hours a day to serve our customers, and so I accumulate a lot of coffee grounds. What's the best way to use these grounds in the garden? Can I overdo it?*

A: Coffee grounds are a fertile source of organic matter and plant food—in fact, they contain about 4 percent nitrogen, 1 percent phosphorus, and 3 percent potassium, giving them an impressive 4-1-3 fertilizer rating, explains Cary Oshins, composting specialist at the Rodale Institute Experimental Farm in Maxatawny, Pennsylvania.

The best way to use them directly, says Oshins, is to spread a layer of grounds on top of the soil and then dig them in. But fresh coffee grounds *can* burn young plants (just like raw manure), so wait about 2 weeks before setting out transplants or sowing seeds in that area, he advises, adding that you can safely work fresh grounds into the soil around *mature, acid-loving* plants such as azaleas, rhododendrons, blueberries, or conifers.

Composting the grounds may be the best option, however, because you can add composted grounds to your garden *any* time without burning plants. They're easy to compost, too. Coffee grounds have a carbon-to-nitrogen ratio of about 20:1, and "that's so close to the ideal ratio of

25 parts carbon to 1 part nitrogen that you can add the grounds to a working compost pile without worrying about upsetting the balance of the pile," explains Oshins.

But yes, it *is* possible to overdo coffee grounds alone— they simply contain too little phosphorus to classify as a "balanced" organic fertilizer. To remedy this, stick to coffee-rich compost, or dig in some bonemeal or rock phosphate when preparing a "black coffee" bed for planting.

The Benefits of Epsom Salts

Q: *I was told that feeding your tomatoes Epsom salts will give you earlier and sweeter tomatoes. Is there anything to this? I haven't tried it because I'm afraid I'll kill my plants.*

A: Epsom salts are magnesium sulfate and magnesium is an essential nutrient for all plants, including tomatoes. *If* your soil lacks magnesium, adding small amounts of Epsom salts could correct the problem. (In acid soils, another way to correct a magnesium deficiency is to use dolomitic limestone, which contains both calcium and magnesium.) But only a soil test can tell you whether your soil is actually deficient in magnesium; if it is, the soil test can also reveal exactly how much fertilizer you should apply in order to correct the condition.

If it turns out that your soil is not low in magnesium, adding Epsom salts could indeed harm, rather than help, your plants. Some soils already contain too much magnesium, and adding more of this nutrient would reduce the availability of other key nutrients, including calcium and potassium, warns soil scientist Garn Wallace, Ph.D., of Wallace Laboratories in El Segundo, California. Excess magnesium also makes heavy clay soils even stickier. And recent research has linked an overabundance of this mineral to the tomato disorders white core (hard white sections inside the fruit) and yellow eye (a yellow halo around the stem scar).

Before you apply special fertilizers of any kind, first test the soil to determine what it needs (or does not need). Soil tests are inexpensive; many states provide testing services for less than $10. (Check with your local cooperative extension office for details.) After you've corrected the deficiency, use compost routinely to maintain the proper nutrient levels. "Because compost is made from decomposed plants and animals, it contains all necessary nutrients in the right proportions," Dr. Wallace says. "And that perfect balance is what will make your plants grow best, giving you early harvests of sweet, tasty tomatoes."

Foliar Feeding Time

Q: *When is the best (and worst) time to apply a foliar spray? How should it be applied to minimize dripping and splashing? Are foliar sprays worth the potential damage they might cause in your garden?*

A: You should spray liquid fertilizer solutions (fish emulsion, seaweed, etc.) in late evening or early morning when temperatures are cool. Plants absorb these liquids through their stomata, porelike openings on their leaves that close up during the heat of midday.

Spray the solution onto plants in as fine a mist as possible. There shouldn't be much dripping, and there really shouldn't be *any* significant splashing when you use a sprayer.

A wetting agent or "sticker-spreader" added to a foliar solution will help it stay on the plant's leaves longer, thus increasing absorption. You can make your own by adding a teaspoon or so of sugar, molasses, soy oil, or corn oil per gallon of mixed fertilizer solution. In addition to helping the

Put compost at the top of your list of ingredients for potting up container gardens and houseplants. Adding compost to potting soil mixes provides a steady stream of nutrients that are released slowly over a long period of time. Plus, compost won't burn the roots or cause major salt buildups the way synthetic chemical fertilizers can. Whenever you pot up a new plant or repot old ones, add 1 part compost for every 3 or 4 parts potting soil.

spray adhere longer to the leaves, the sugar and molasses are both sources of trace minerals that will add to the fertilizing potential of your foliar spray, explains Amigo Bob Cantisano of Organic Ag Advisors in Colfax, California. You can also buy commercial sticker-spreader products from a mail-order source like Peaceful Valley Farm Supply (see "Resources" on page 234).

Your remark about "potential damage" confuses us. Are you concerned about the potential for overfeeding? Foliar feeding could theoretically promote excessive growth, but that would be unlikely. If you mixed too concentrated a solution, it could possibly burn foliage, especially if temperatures get red hot right after you apply it. But there's essentially no risk with proper use. Just remember that any added fertilizer of any kind, applied in any form, is no substitute for good, rich, fertile, compost-amended soil.

Indoor Dining

Q: *I would like some advice on recipes for organic fertilizers for houseplants. The commercial ones available are kind of expensive. I thought of mixing bonemeal and bloodmeal, but I am not sure of the ratios or of what other materials I could use to make a balanced plant food. Any suggestions?*

A: Our first suggestion: Don't feed your houseplants with anything while they're dormant—they aren't actively growing in winter and any added nutrients will hang around in the soil as a buildup of mineral salts. However, your houseplants will welcome a nice organic breakfast when they wake up to brighter, longer, and warmer days of spring and start putting on new leaves and length.

One part bloodmeal, one part bonemeal, and two parts wood ashes will supply a good balance of nutrients to your houseplants, but Steve Rioch, soil consultant (tester and recommender) at Timberleaf Farms in Albany, Ohio, warns that you'll have to use it very sparingly—the bloodmeal will make the mix very hot. Scratch small amounts of the mix into the surface of your potting soil or add a few teaspoons to new soil when you repot.

Bloodmeal is about 15 percent nitrogen, bonemeal is about 21 percent phosphorus, and wood ashes are about 7 percent potassium. Put them all together and you get an organic fertilizer supplying nitrogen, phosphorus, and potassium at a ratio of about 5-6-4.

To ensure that your plants get enough nitrogen, give them an occasional extra watering with some fish emulsion. If you shop around, you should be able to buy a gallon of the concentrated-fish stuff for about $10. Diluted, this will last for years. Yes, fish emulsion does smell, even if the label says it's deodorized—so apply it once every 2 weeks when your plants are outside for the summer (or make your solution half as strong and use it twice as often). In fact, if your plants are low-light, nonflowering varieties, fish emulsion (which is about 5-2-2) may supply everything they need.

Victoria Jahn, associate information director at the Brooklyn Botanic Garden, prefers liquid fertilizers for houseplants because you can adjust the application rate when you need to. For example, if the weather turns unseasonably cool and cloudy and the plant enters an unexpected holding pattern or if you're having a scale problem and you want to reduce the amount of nitrogen going into plants, you can simply use a weaker solution. If you want more blooms or if the weather is perfect and your plants are growing strong, you can easily increase the strength.

How can you tell when your indoor plants need special nutrients? Here's a troubleshooting guide: Lack of nitrogen shows up as yellow lower leaves, an overall light green color, or stunted growth; plants lacking phosphorus will have red, purple, or very dark green foliage and their growth will be stunted; too little potassium—the tips and edges of leaves will turn yellow then brown, or the plants will have weak stems.

And don't ignore compost. Scratch an occasional ½ inch layer of the finished product into the surface of your houseplants' soil, add some compost to your repotting soil, or just water your plants regularly with compost tea. To make such a tea, steep a cloth bag full of compost in a bucket of water for a couple of weeks until the water turns brown.

And finally, if this all sounds too complicated, don't worry—according to the advice of many experts, overfertilization kills more plants than underfertilization.

Using the Right Lime

Q: *I read some advice in a gardening book that's counter to what I've been doing. It said "spread lime on the soil surface after digging; do not dig it in and try not to spread lime after manuring the soil." Is this correct?*

A: The author of the book was probably writing about burned lime (a.k.a. quicklime) or slaked lime (a.k.a. hydrated lime), which no organic gardener would want to use, says Steve Rioch, soil consultant at Timberleaf Farms in Albany, Ohio.

Those materials started out as mined limestone that was then heated to make its calcium more readily available. (Calcium is the component of lime that helps raise a soil's pH to make it less acidic.) But these heated forms of lime are caustic (a.k.a. dangerous) and difficult to work with. The reason you wouldn't want to dig the stuff into recently manured soil is that the burned or slaked lime can kill the microbial life in the manure.

It's *much* more environmentally benign (and safer to *you*) to just use mined lime. You can use finely ground limestone (which raises pH fairly quickly) or crushed limestone, neither of which will harm soil life. And the *better* you mix ground limestone in with your soil, the more effective it will be.

Kelp Can Help, If You're Careful

Q: *Can I use raw kelp as a fertilizer? How can I make a liquid fertilizer from kelp?*

A: Yes, you can use kelp as a fertilizer, with a few cautions. When using the sea plant as a soil amendment, you risk a toxic salt problem at application rates over 1.38 pounds per square foot, warns Wayne D. Temple, researcher with the University of British Columbia. "In areas that don't receive a lot of precipitation, you could experience a buildup of salt," he says. But if you live in an area of high rainfall, the sea salts present generally leach out over the winter.

If you prefer to use kelp as a foliar spray, apply a little bit often for best results. Temple recommends diluting concentrates to 1:200 or 1:400, and spraying until plants are dripping. Start with seedlings, and spray every 2 weeks up to four applications during the growing season.

"The active constituent of seaweed is not well known," Temple says. "Sometimes foliar feeding works, sometimes it doesn't." He adds that foliar feeding works best on broadleaf crops such as beans and tomatoes. In one study, Temple found foliar feeding increased bean yields by 24 percent.

If harvesting your own kelp, Temple says to be sure to pick fresh plants, not ones that have been rotting on the beach. The best time to harvest is early spring or late fall. Rinse to remove any sand or debris.

Seaweed is hard to grind up to make a foliar spray, Temple says. For Seaspray, the commercial product that he developed, the kelp undergoes a process similar to homogenization. *Organic Gardening* magazine recommended (more than two decades ago) that readers try chopping seaweed in a large, old-fashioned food grinder, adding 2 pounds of the ground seaweed to 1 gallon of hot water, and letting it steep overnight. Temple said that the recommendation is not a bad idea, but said you probably don't have to use hot water. "Experiment with the results," he says. "Don't apply it to everything."

E. Coli and Garden Manures

Q: *I enjoy raising organic fruits and vegetables, which I feel are healthier than the produce sold at grocery stores. But am I putting my family at risk of contacting the dreaded* E. coli *bacteria by using manure (cow and rabbit) to fertilize my gardens? Are some manures less likely to contain* E. coli *than others?*

A: The best way to avoid *E. coli* problems is to thoroughly compost any manure before using it and to practice cleanliness in the garden. The high heat of an actively "cooking" compost pile (use a compost thermometer to make sure your pile reaches 140° to 160°F) will kill most *E. coli* and other pathogens, explains Cary Oshins, compost specialist at the Rodale Institute Experimental Farm in Maxatawny, Pennsylvania. Any surviving disease organisms will be finished off by the beneficial bacteria that thrive during the compost curing stage, he adds.

To make certain you achieve complete composting, "keep the pile moist [as wet as a wrung-out sponge] and well ventilated, and turn it at least once or twice," advises Oshins, who explains that "the average time to finished compost with such a pile will be about 4 months during the summer and 8 months during the fall and winter. The finished compost," he adds, "should be dark and crumbly and have an earthy odor." It should not have any kind of manure smell, and you shouldn't be able to recognize any of the original ingredients.

And follow cleanliness guidelines when working with manure or compost made with manure: Wash your hands before touching food or food plants; don't wear your gardening clothes into the kitchen to cook; and thoroughly wash all produce you grow or buy.

By the way, the "dreaded E. coli" you refer to is probably the newly discovered *Escherichia coli* 0157: H7 strain. Most *E. coli* strains are benign—we all carry some around in our guts and *E. coli* of one form or another is ubiquitous in the environment. But *E. coli* 0157: H7 is a nasty strain that has been linked with human illness and even some deaths. It has been found in the guts of healthy cows, deer, and elk, and occasionally in sheep, but it has never been found in rabbits, reports Bob Howard, special assistant to the director of the National Center for Infectious Disease. However, any animal can spread the bacteria by ingesting and then excreting it in its manure.

Even flies can carry *E. coli,* reports Brad Bosworth, Ph.D., a scientist with the USDA Agricultural Research Service National Animal Disease Center, so keep those airborne nasties out of the kitchen and away from food.

Bunny Booster

Q: *Please tell me whether rabbit manure is good for fertilizing gardens. One of my neighbors said it was too acidic. Another neighbor said it was no good. A third neighbor, who raises rabbits, spread the manure*

CHECK IT OUT!

Before you reach for the fertilizer, be sure to have your soil tested. The test results will reveal whether your soil has a pH problem or possibly a nutrient imbalance. Factors like the soil's pH and the way certain nutrients react together can dramatically affect the way plant roots are able to absorb the nutrients that are in the soil. You can have a basic soil test done through your state's cooperative extension service for a nominal fee. You'll find their number listed under the county agencies in your telephone directory.

on my garden. So far, everything is growing well, but the first neighbor said I shouldn't add any more for a while. What do you think?

A: Rabbit manure is an *excellent* source of garden nutrients. It has an approximate value of 3.7 percent nitrogen, 1.3 percent phosphorus, and 3.5 percent potassium, which compares favorably to poultry manure (which contains about 4.7 percent nitrogen, 1.5 percent phosphorus, and 1 percent potassium).

What's more, Peter R. Cheeke, Ph.D., professor of animal nutrition at Oregon State University, notes that rabbits are herbivores whose manure contains lots of undigested fiber that improves soil texture *and* adds lots of organic matter. (And rabbit manure has an *alkaline* pH, not an acid one, adds Dr. Cheeke.)

Sure, you can overdo *any* fertilizer (except maybe compost), but a thin layer of rabbit manure once or twice a year is not too much. As with any manure, you'll get the best results if you compost or age it for several months before you spread it.

Oysters on the Rocks

Q: *I read with great interest the article on the potential benefits of rock dust in the garden in an old issue of* Organic Gardening *magazine. Would the ground oyster shells that you can buy at a feed store serve the same purpose?*

A: Adding ground oyster shells with their high levels of calcium (34 percent) would be a good substitute for adding ground limestone to your soil, says Robert Parnes, Ph.D., author of *Fertile Soil: A Grower's Guide to Organic & Inorganic Fertilizers* (AgAccess Publications, 1990). But before you add either, you need to have your soil tested. These soil additives will change your soil's pH, and you don't want to do that in the wrong direction. Contact your local cooperative extension office for test details; you'll find their number listed in the county offices section of your phone book.

Ground oyster shells and limestone will raise a soil's pH level; that is, make it less acidic. If your soil's pH is already on the alkaline side (higher than 7.0), you don't want to make it more so. (The most fertile soil generally has a pH range of 6.3 to 6.8.) If your soil is extremely acidic (a low pH), go right ahead and add some calcium-rich amendments. That low pH is limiting the biological activity in your soil.

How fast oyster shells will change soil pH depends on how finely they are ground, so go for dusty if you have a choice. And you get a bonus—the shells will probably add a few minerals other than calcium to your soil mix as well, Dr. Parnes says.

Enzymes, Anyone?

Q: *I know of several companies selling enzymes they say will increase crop production and activate compost. Are these products worth the money?*

A: Maybe, maybe not. It depends on what your soil or compost pile needs. These natural chemical compounds produced by bacteria are not plant foods, but catalysts—they prompt chemical reactions that unlock nutrients from the organic and inorganic components of soil. They mostly do so in order that these nutrients can be absorbed by the bacteria that produced the enzymes. But this unlocking also benefits nearby plants.

If your soil is badly depleted or compacted, and your compost pile is cold, these products might boost biological activity, but they are not a substitute for good management practices. (And be aware that enzymes break down organic matter; so your soil will need more organic matter if you use enzymes.)

GENERAL SOIL CARE

Ready, Set, Rotate

Q: *Is there a tried and true method of crop rotation? I live in Zone 9 and plant both spring and fall crops in my garden.*

A: Only one fundamental rule applies to crop rotation, says Pat Michalak, an integrated pest management (IPM) consultant who has written about pest and disease control (and other garden topics) for Rodale: "Change!"

"Every time you plant a crop in a certain spot, make sure it belongs to a different botanical family than what was growing there before," she advises. The main families and their members are: crucifers (broccoli, brussels sprouts, cabbage, cauliflower, kale, radishes, turnips); curcurbits (cucumbers, melons, squash, pumpkins); legumes (peas, beans, clovers, vetches); grains (wheat, oats, rye, corn); alliums (onions, garlic, leeks); nightshades (eggplants, potatoes, tomatoes, peppers); and umbels (carrots, parsley, parsnips, rutabagas, dill, fennel).

For added insurance, you can also categorize plants as "roots," "leaves," or "fruits," says Michalak. Then each time you plant, change the family *and* the category; don't follow a root with a root, a leafy crop with a leafy crop, or a fruiting crop (like a tomato or a string bean) with another fruiting crop. The longer you can keep the same family and plant type out of the same spot, the better. (Crop rotation breaks the continuing cycle of pests and diseases that can occur when a particular type of plant is put repeatedly in the same spot in the garden. Rotation also varies the nutrient demands on your plots of soil.)

"Rotation can be as complicated or as simple as you like," explains Michalak, who expands her one-word rule into four simple steps:

STEP 1: Build the soil with a soil-improving cover crop.

STEP 2: Follow the cover crop with a heavy feeder that's not in the same family.

STEP 3: Follow that heavy feeder with a light feeder, also not from the same family.

STEP 4: Repeat.

"If you can't change the family from season to season (say you have a very small garden and *only* grow tomatoes, for example), change the variety," she suggests, "and change the kind of mulch you use and the kind of cover crop you grow and your methods of pest control. Always be sure to change *something* within the system every time you plant."

Cover crops are an extremely important part of a rotation plan in hot clime gardens such as yours because organic matter practically evaporates in your light soils and high temperatures.

The Forbidden Planting

Q: *I recently moved and just discovered that the sunny part of the yard where I planned to put the garden is over the septic system drain field. Can I grow anything other than a lawn over top of it?*

A: Nope. "We don't recommend planting much more than grass over a drain field," says John Eliasson, wastewater management specialist for the Washington State Department of Health.

Most drain fields consist of pipes embedded in gravel-filled trenches that can sometimes be positioned less than

1 foot below the surface of the soil. Normal garden activities such as tilling and irrigation could cause costly (and nasty) damage to shallow drain fields, warns Eliasson. And don't even *think* about eating anything grown on top of a drain field. "There are a number of diseases that could be transmitted from the sewage," he stresses.

Those prohibitions go double for sand-mound–style septic systems, which are even more easily disturbed. Recommendations about what can be planted over septic systems are pretty strict, says Eliasson, and some municipalities might have even *stricter* regulations than Washington State's. Readers should check with their local health department before planting *anything* other than grass atop a drain field.

Keep Your Garden Dry

Q: *My garden is situated in a low area, where the soil stays moist even during very dry seasons. During really wet weather, any fruit that comes in contact with the ground rots. Beans develop rust and immature summer squash, carrots, cabbage, tomatoes, and onions rot. Some old-timers have suggested spraying the entire garden a few times with copper compounds before planting, then covering the entire plot with black plastic. What should I do?*

A: You don't describe your soil, but building up its organic matter and gardening in raised beds should help. Specifically, your drainage will improve and those wet conditions will be minimized, says Jack Lewis, Ph.D., soil scientist at the USDA's Agricultural Research Service Plant Diseases Biocontrol Laboratory. "If the ground is sodden, you will get rots," he says.

To get the best results from additional organic matter, spread a couple inches of aged compost, aged manure, or shredded leaves over your garden, then dig or till it all into the top layer of your soil. Remember that soil organisms break organic matter down continually, so keep adding more on a regular basis. You can also improve your soil structure by growing some cover crops, such as rye or hairy vetch, this fall.

Raised beds will improve drainage, protect the soil from compaction, and improve root health. Your soil situation sounds pretty severe, so you may also need to add sand to improve your drainage enough (especially if your soil is heavy clay).

As an interim solution, try putting down a straw mulch around your plants. Its surface will dry quickly after rain and keep fruits and vegetables from coming in contact with the ground. The mulch may slow some of the contamination that is occurring, but it can't stop the organisms living in the ground from attacking your plants' roots.

Copper is a very strong fungicide that kills beneficial organisms as well as foes. Dr. Lewis warns that turning to such a solution could make your soil toxic.

Healthy Soil, Healthy People

Q: *We grow a lot of our own produce, but I'm wondering whether it is as nutritious as it could be. I've heard that agricultural land becomes severely depleted of minerals within 10 to 15 years. And our soil here in northeast Iowa doesn't naturally contain selenium—an important mineral for good health. Are there amendments that could help make our soil (and the produce we grow in it) more nutritionally balanced?*

A: Yes, soils *do* gradually lose minerals that veggies take up and that are important for good health. Soils can also be naturally deficient in minerals—your soil, for instance, doesn't have selenium because the underlying rocks in your region contain very little selenium, explains Randy Killorn, Ph.D., extension agronomist at Iowa State University.

Your first step toward improving your soil's health is to have your soil tested; that way you'll know *exactly* what minerals it contains and lacks. Most state labs offer a basic soil test for a nominal fee and will test your micronutrients (zinc, iron, boron, etc.) for a few dollars more. (Contact your local cooperative extension office for details.) Wallace Laboratories, a private lab located at 365 Coral Circle, El Segundo, CA 90245, tests for selenium.

But healthy soil contains more than just a good mix of minerals, of course. Healthy soil is also biologically active, adds Laurie Drinkwater, Ph.D., director of the Rodale Institute's Soil Health Initiative. (The Institute, a nonprofit organization, has recently renewed its mission to champion the connection between soil, food, and human health.) A healthy soil, she explains, is home to critters like earthworms, beneficial nematodes, mites, and microbes. It is also porous, crumbly, and airy, she says.

The best way to improve the *overall* health of your soil, says Dr. Drinkwater, is to add lots of organic matter like compost, chopped-up cover crops (especially legumes, which have the ability to manufacture their own plant-feeding nitrogen from the air), and organic fertilizers like composted manure, seafood wastes, and fish and seaweed preparations. These will feed the tiny creatures that live in the soil, who will in turn decompose the organic matter, transforming it into substances that feed the plants, which in turn feed you.

A specific remedy for your selenium deficiency: Look for a well-managed cattle or dairy farm in your area. It's common practice for animals in selenium-deficient areas to be fed supplements, since they aren't getting what they need from locally grown grains and grass. Adding their "enriched" manure to your compost pile would be a safe and effective way to get selenium into your soil, suggests Ivan Palmer, Ph.D., chemistry professor and selenium researcher at South Dakota University.

Of Tillers and Worms

Q: *We bought a mini-tiller this year and are excited about using it, but we are also concerned about the impact it will have on our earthworm population. Our yard is blessed with millions of earthworms—how can we minimize damage to them? Would it help to let the soil dry out prior to tilling, thus driving the earthworms deeper below the surface?*

A: Yes, allowing your soil to dry out will encourage the earthworms to move deeper and, consequently, out of the way of the tiller's tines. "Earthworms like cool, damp, dark conditions," says Matthew Werner, Ph.D., soil ecology specialist at the Center for Agroecology and Sustainable Food Systems at the University of California in Santa Cruz. While waiting for warm, sunny weather, rake the old mulch off of the soil surface. This will help dry the soil *and* remove a source of food (the decaying organic matter) for the earthworms, which also will help force them deeper into the soil, explains Dr. Werner. (And you should always till when your soil is on the dry side to begin with; *never* till in *wet* soil, say the experts.) But when you're *not* tilling (or don't plan to), make those worms feel at home by covering the surface of the soil with chopped leaf litter, digging in some aged manure, and, of course, avoiding chemicals, notes Dr. Werner. He adds that, for the record, cutting a worm in half—with any implement—will *not* get you two! "If a worm *does* get chopped up, it will either die or regenerate one part of its body—sometimes it's the tail end and sometimes it's the head—but cutting a worm in two *doesn't* result in two worms," he says.

Pea Predicament

Q: *Since I began using purple vetch as a cover crop and mulch in my garden 3 years ago, my soil has changed from red clay to a deep, rich, and almost granular loam. But I'm worried: If I plant my English and sugar snap peas in that soil, could I be putting them at risk for diseases carried by the vetch (since all are legumes)?*

A: Yes, pests and diseases can build up wherever the same crop—or a related one—is planted in the same spot year after year. And specific to your case, "root rot, a disease that builds up in the soil, can develop by following a legume cover crop [such as purple vetch] with a legume food crop [such as peas]," states Earl T. Gritton, Ph.D., a professor emeritus of agronomy at the University of Wisconsin, where he worked on the pea improvement program. Vetches also harbor viruses that could be spread to your pea plants by aphids, he adds, so don't grow those two legumes at the same time.

And while you seem to have had success in improving your soil with just that vetch cover crop so far, you are taking a chance by not mixing things up from time to time. To decrease the risk of disease, try rye, wheat, oats, or grasses as cover crops in the spots where you intend to plant peas or beans.

Three Super Soil Mixes

Q: *I once read in Organic Gardening magazine a "recipe" for the best potting material ever developed by a university. Do you have that recipe?*

A: You're probably thinking of a version of "the Cornell Mix," which was formulated in the early 1970s by horticulturists at Cornell University. Cornell's recipe—designed to provide a consistently high-quality, lightweight growing medium for seedlings and transplants—included a commercial chemical fertilizer. This organic version relies on organic fertilizers instead of chemicals to supply the needed nitrogen, phosphorus, and potassium: 1 bushel shredded peat, 1 bushel perlite or vermiculite, ½ cup ground limestone, 1 cup blood meal, 1 cup colloidal phosphate, and 1 cup greensand.

You could also use compost to supply the nutrients. The Rodale Institute Experimental Farm in Maxatawny, Pennsylvania, uses a compost-based seed-starting mix similar to this: 4 parts very old, well-finished, and finely screened compost, 1 part vermiculite, 1 part perlite, and 2 parts peat.

And if you want a seed-starting mix with fewer purchased ingredients, here's one from the Center for Agroecology and Sustainable Food Systems at the University of California at Santa Cruz: 3 parts well-finished, finely screened compost, 2 parts loamy garden soil, 1 part builder's (not beach) sand, and 1 to 2 parts well-rotted leaf mold.

Chapter

PESTS

Your garden is a tempting invitation to animal and insect pests to have a snack or two! So what do you do about the caterpillars eating your cabbage, the voles decimating your bulbs, and those deer that eat, well, everything? You'll find the solutions to these common pest problems (and some uncommon ones) right here.

BATTLING INSECTS
Aphids, Aphids Everywhere

Q: *The only thing that stops me from growing beautiful cauliflower and broccoli is the large number of aphids that attach themselves under, around, and inside the florets. How can I get rid of these pests organically?*

A: The first step in *preventing* aphids from getting a toehold in your crucifers is to give your broccoli and cauliflower plants plenty of room, explains Ed Lidzbarski of E. R. & Son Farm in Jamesburg, New Jersey. Aphids thrive in closed, damp environments where they find protection from wind and rain.

Lidzbarski grows his broccoli and cauliflower in rows that are a wide 3 feet apart, with the broccoli plants themselves an extra generous 3 feet apart in the row and cauliflower plants 2 feet apart. "Even if one or two plants *do* become infected with aphids, the aphids don't spread to the other plants," he adds.

If aphids *do* show up, wash them off the plants with a strong spray of water. Any that survive the force of water won't crawl back, says Bruce Marek of Old Hook Farm in Emerson, New Jersey. Just be sure to direct the spray of water to the *underside* of the leaves and into all the little nooks and crannies of your plants where aphids like to hide.

And don't forget beneficial insects. The larvae of both lacewings and ladybugs will eat *lots* of aphids for you;

attract the adult beneficials by planting dill, fennel, carrots, and parsley and by letting them flower (with carrots, that will be in their *second* year, so don't pull them up). The flowers of these plants provide nectar and pollen for the beneficials.

Yellow Jacket, Yellow Jacket, Fly Away Home

Q: *The worst pests around my house are some kind of bee or wasp I call "garbage bees" because they are always buzzing around the garbage cans in parks. They also seem attracted to sweaty people working in the garden, and by the end of summer it's impossible to go outside with any food because it attracts them. I have small children, and these things are a hazard. Is there an organic way to get rid of them or at least discourage them?*

A: Sounds like you're being held hostage by yellow jackets—a general term used to describe a group of aggressive, scavenging hornets and wasps that nest in holes in the ground. First the good news—just because they're hanging around your house one year doesn't mean that they'll be back the next. Queens start new colonies from scratch every spring.

If new nests *are* built in your yard, you should be able to find the exact location by watching the yellow jackets fly in and out of them. You'll be able to spot these flying tigers most easily when the angle of the sun is low, around 9 A.M. and 3 P.M., says John F. MacDonald, Ph.D., associate professor of entomology at Purdue University.

Once you locate the nests, you can significantly reduce yellow-jacket numbers by placing traps around them. One such trap, the Rescue Reusable Yellow-Jacket Trap (available at home and garden centers), is a sturdy plastic cylinder that contains an attractant that the wasps find irresistible. Once the yellow jackets find their way into the cone, they can't get back out. Stephanie Cates, sales manager at Sterling International, Rescue's manufacturer, recommends placing the traps around the perimeter of your garden early in the spring when the temperatures reach 70°F consistently. "If you can catch the queens before they begin to make their nests, you can often prevent larger infestations later in the season."

Empty the traps periodically, then wash them with soap and water before you put them away for the year. (Yellow-jacket populations reach their peak during the late summer and early fall.) In addition to traps, you can help discourage yellow jackets from joining your family picnics by keeping garbage cans tightly covered and by serving sodas and other sweet beverages in cups with lids.

Beat the Bean Beetles

Q: *Last summer a yellow and black spotted bug ate our string-bean plants bare. The bug's larva was fuzzy and yellow. What is it, and what can I do about it?*

A: It's the Mexican bean beetle. Adult beetles spend the winter in litter or brush around the garden. When the weather warms up to the 60s in spring, the beetles fly to young bean plants and lay eggs. The eggs hatch in 5 to 14 days (depending on how warm it is) into those fuzzy little larvae you saw, and those voracious eaters feed on bean leaves for 2 or 3 weeks, then pupate on the leaves. Adults emerge from the pupae and start eating *more* bean leaves.

In general, you can lessen the damage if you plant a new row of beans every couple of weeks throughout the season (which you should do anyway to extend the harvest). It takes awhile for bean beetle populations to build up in a patch, so you should be able to take quite a few pickings before they completely destroy the leaves. When a patch *does* become infested, just pull it all up, destroy it, and move on to the next crop.

Or grow your beans under floating row covers. Tuck the cover into place as soon as the seeds are in the ground. Remember to leave plenty of room for the beans to reach their full bush size—place a few stakes in there at the right height and keep those edges sealed. Keep the cover over the plants until the beans are ready to pick.

On the East Coast, spined soldier bugs feed on Mexican bean beetle eggs and larvae, as do some ladybugs. You can bring native soldier bugs into your garden with the Rescue lure, available directly from Sterling International, P.O. Box 220, Liberty, VA 99019; (800) 666-6766; fax: (509) 928-7313; Web site: www.rescue.com.

Protecting Potatoes

Q: *I planted four long rows of potatoes last year, and I wish I had a nickel for every Colorado potato beetle I picked off them. They never quit. I even tried making "bug juice" (whizzing a bunch of pest insects in a blender with a pint of water, straining and spraying this mixture on the plant under attack in the belief that it would repel similar pests), but it didn't help. What else can I do?*

A: You can try trench warfare. Simple trenches dug around a potato patch have been shown to substantially reduce the number of beetles on the potatoes in that patch. Agriculture Canada researchers at Fredericton in New

Brunswick, led by Gilles Boitreu, Ph.D., were able to cut beetle numbers by 90 percent with this technique. Here's how to do it in your garden.

Those loathsome beetles spend the winter in warm south- or west-facing woods, hedgerows, and similar areas close to last year's potato patch. So plant *this* year's potato patch *as close to these suspected overwintering sites as possible.* Then dig a trench that's at least 1 foot deep (and about 1 foot wide at the top), and line that trench with black plastic.

Finally, sprinkle dust lightly over the entire trench—this dust will gum up the beetles' feet and make it impossible for them to crawl out of the trench. After it rains, renew the dust.

When the Colorado potato beetles begin to wake up in spring, they'll start to crawl toward your potato patch, so the closer you place your trench to their overwintering site, the more beetles will fall into the trench. And once those beetles slide down that plastic, they can't get out again, especially if the plastic is smooth, dry, dusty, and without wrinkles.

Some beetles *will* try to fly out of the trench, but the researchers observed that very few actually made it out; they usually crashed into the walls of the trench and slid back down to the bottom, where they died of dehydration in about a week. (When building your trap, make small holes in the plastic at the bottom of the trench about every foot so that rainwater can drain out.)

These trenches will *also* work to trap beetles crawling *out* of your potato patch in the fall as they make their way toward those overwintering sites. Be sure to keep your trench edges weed-free, so that the beetles will fall in more readily.

Too late to trench? Use BT *(Bacillus thuringiensis)*, a naturally occurring bacterium that's only toxic to caterpillars. To battle Colorado potato beetles, you want the "San Diego" strain; *BT* var. *San Diego* (the official wording) will kill beetles that munch on potato plants where you've applied BT, but it won't harm any other creatures (including you) and doesn't affect the potatoes themselves at all.

Apply it to your potato plants as soon as you see newly hatched larvae crawling around (they look like fat little orange slugs). You can buy BT products in garden centers.

Close Encounters of the Ladybug Kind

Q: *We have a terrible problem with ladybugs in western Tennessee. They start coming into our houses in October, and we see them inside all winter. Just when we think we've gotten rid of them all, we find more. Where did so many come from?*

A: These ladybugs (which are aphid-eating beneficials) are just doing what comes naturally—meeting up with other ladybugs and looking for a warm place to spend the winter.

"Ladybugs will often gather on the west side of a house in the warm afternoon sun in fall," says Frank A. Hale, Ph.D., an entomologist with the University of Tennessee's agricultural extension service. From there they often seek shelter in the leaf litter around the base of the house while looking for a cozy spot to hibernate, and from there it's just a short crawl into your home via tiny cracks, heating ducts, and such.

"Inspect the outside of your house and caulk any holes and cracks," suggests Dr. Hale, who adds that if ladybugs are getting in, so is cold air, raising your heating bill. If you do find ladybugs inside, though, please don't kill them! Just sweep them into dustpans and "throw them into your garden instead," says Dr. Hale.

Or save them in your refrigerator until spring, says Ken Hagen, Ph.D., entomology professor emeritus at the University of California's Laboratory of Biological Control.

Gather up any you find by gently nudging them onto a small piece of paper. Then place them in a box or jar with air holes in the lid (and with something inside for them to climb on), and store the container in the refrigerator, says Dr. Hagen, a prominent ladybug authority.

"They will live on their stored fat over the winter, but they need occasional water," he explains. Every week or so, take the container out of the refrigerator, and sprinkle a little water inside. The warm temperatures outside the fridge will wake the beetles up, and they'll drink the water. After a half hour or so, put the container back in the fridge. (Always keep the container out of direct sun, and don't let it sit in a warm room very long.) Release your pest patrol in the spring into a wet garden in the evening after daytime temperatures remain consistently above 55°F. You'll need to have herbs or similar plants in flower to provide pollen for the ladybugs to eat until they find pests to picnic on.

Punctured Peppers

Q: My sweet bell peppers are often ruined by the time they turn red. The fruits have a rotten area on the inside, and on the outside, there's a pinhole opening that I assume was made by some insect. Can you tell me what the insect is and how I can control it?

A: Despite the name, the culprit is probably the European corn borer because in addition to corn, this voracious pest also dines on a host of other vegetables, including peppers, beans, beets, cabbage, celery, eggplant, okra, tomatoes, and potatoes, explains Jerry Ghidiu, Ph.D., extension entomologist at Rutgers University in New Jersey.

Female moths (pale yellowish brown, about 1 inch across) lay their eggs on the pepper fruit or plant. When the eggs hatch, larvae enter the pepper under the plug where the stem meets the fruit. The larvae feed on the inside of the pepper awhile, then exit through holes that they make in a side wall. The damage to the pepper lets in air, water, fungus, and bacteria and causes the fruit to rot and turn red prematurely, says Dr. Ghidiu.

Bacillus thuringiensis var. *kurstaki,* a naturally occurring bacteria that kills caterpillars but doesn't harm other creatures, is effective against European corn borer larvae on corn. But with peppers, the larvae feed *inside* the pepper fruit, where the BT can't reach them.

The best way to protect your peppers from corn borer damage is to cover the plants with a floating row cover by mid-May, when borer adults start laying eggs, suggests Dr. Ghidiu. (Peppers pollinate themselves, so you don't have to lift the cover to let in pollinating insects, the way you do with some other crops.) Also, since borer larvae overwinter in corn and other hollow plant stalks, remove and destroy all such debris after harvest in the fall.

Rhododendron Rescue

Q: *I have beautiful rhododendrons but they're all infested with borers. Do you have any ideas on how to save them organically?*

A: The rhododendron borer is the larval stage of a clear-winged moth. The larvae tunnel into the bark and wood of the rhododendron, causing the decline of the plant. While nematodes haven't been tested specifically on rhododendron borers, they have been used successfully (achieving up to 88 percent control) on other clear-winged moth larvae in similar situations, reveals Debbie Smith-Fiola, an extension agent and pest management specialist with the Rutgers Cooperative Extension of Ocean County, New Jersey.

The trick is to get the nematodes into the borer tunnels and cracks, which should be visible on the bark. First, wet the bark with plain water, then apply the nematode solution to the bark using a low-pressure sprayer. If the nematodes survive (they require a moist, cool, and dark environment, which luckily pretty much describes those borer tunnels), they will attack the larvae. Bright sunlight kills nematodes, so do your spraying in early morning or late evening.

Borer moths lay their eggs on rhododendron shrubs in May and June. The eggs hatch and larvae are active inside the bark from July until moths emerge the following May or June. "The sooner you apply the nematodes the better because little larvae are easier to kill," says Smith-Fiola. (You can order nematodes from various garden supply catalogs, including Gardens Alive!—see "Resources" on page 234.) Other borer battle plans: Prune off and destroy affected branches, and keep shrubs as healthy as possible to better withstand borer attack.

Beat the Bulb Fly

Q: *I've been trying to naturalize narcissus in my garden, but some don't come back the second year. Upon inspecting the failed bulbs, I usually find that they're infested with narcissus bulb fly larvae. The books I've consulted recommend chemicals as a control. Do you know of any alternative solutions?*

A: We can suggest a couple. The first is to only grow *early* varieties—narcissus that flower before the narcissus bulb fly starts flying (check catalog descriptions for early-blooming varieties). Then, when the blooming's done, tuck floating row covers over the plants to keep the fly from laying its eggs in the plants' stems and necks. (The eggs hatch into larvae that tunnel their way into the bulbs to eat and hibernate, as you've discovered.)

And plant (or move) *all* your narcissus into a windy spot. The narcissus bulb fly, which looks like a little bumblebee, is a black sheep relative of the beneficial hoverfly. Both are syrphid flies, and both spend a lot of time hovering about. If a nice stiff breeze frequently visits your narcissus patch, narcissus bulb flies are much less likely to do any damage. "Narcissus bulb fly damage doesn't seem to be as severe in windy areas," says Art Antonelli, Ph.D., Washington State University extension entomologist, "because syrphids don't fly too well in the wind."

Keeping Maggots out of the Onions

Q: *Why do my 2-inch-tall onion plants turn yellow and then just get worse, to the point where the bulbs become soft and rotten?*

A: Sounds like your young onion plants are plagued by the onion maggot (*Hylemya antiqua*). The white larva crawls down the plant and tunnels into the bulb, causing the plant to turn yellow and wilt.

"Onion maggots are one of the worst pests to deal with organically," says Bryan Frazer, entomologist for Agriculture Canada in Vancouver. The key to avoiding onion maggot damage is prevention because once maggots infest a crop, there is no reliable way to control them.

"Get onions in the ground as soon as you can to avoid egg-laying flies," Frazer says. "The first generation of adult flies emerges when dandelions bloom." Try raised beds,

CHECK IT OUT!

A strong spray of water from your garden hose will wash off many pests and works especially well for controlling aphids and spider mites. In fact, researchers at Texas A&M University reduced damage from these two pests by as much as 90 percent by spraying water through a special watering wand. You can get good results at home even without a special wand. Simply attach a nozzle to your hose or use your thumb to increase the water pressure and wash the plants thoroughly.

which could give a 2- to 3-week head start, Frazer adds, and use sets rather than seed. Also, don't plant onions where you've previously had onions, leeks, garlic, or other alliums—the pests' pupae overwinter in the soil. Clean up or till under crop residue immediately after harvest.

Frazer also recommends putting screening, such as row covers or even a window screen fixed to a wooden box, over onions immediately after planting. "Onion flies, which function by sense of smell, will come in at germination and lay eggs before the plants even break the soil surface," says Bob Vernon, Ph.D., also with Agriculture Canada. Choose row covers that are an ultraviolet radiation-reflective color such as white, Vernon says, to help repel flies. Extend the cover at least 6 inches to each side of the row to prevent flies from getting at the sides of tender onion plants to lay their eggs. Those row covers also will heat the soil and keep your plants warmer, allowing you to plant earlier and miss the heaviest onslaught of onion maggots. Covers can be removed in late June or early July, when plants have grown big enough to tolerate damage.

As a last resort, you may also want to try applying beneficial nematodes that will attack onion maggots. Vernon reports mixed results in trials using this method of control.

Widespread Whiteflies

Q: *My entire yard is covered with whiteflies, even the grass. I've tried everything except sticky traps because I can't find them. Please help me find a solution before my entire yard is destroyed.*

Q: *I'm having trouble with whiteflies that live in my plants. We started to notice this insect in July; it destroyed tomatoes, cucumbers, squash, and others. It seems to cause the plants to wilt.*

A: Whiteflies are found almost everywhere, and they attack hundreds of kinds of plants. When they feed, they suck the juices out of leaves, spreading viruses and other diseases as they go, *and* their excretions make plants sticky, moldy, and extremely unattractive.

Fortunately, you have a bunch of remedies to choose from. Here's the recipe for an inexpensive do-it-yourself whitefly spray developed by the USDA: Add 1 tablespoon of insecticidal soap to 1 cup of vegetable oil (peanut, safflower, corn, soybean, or sunflower); shake well, and add 1 to 2 teaspoons of this mix to 1 cup of water. Spray this diluted solution directly onto the insects every 7 to 10 days until you get the problem under control. Be sure to spray the undersides of the leaves, too—the solution has to come in contact with the insects to be effective.

USDA researchers found that this spray worked well on whiteflies that were attacking carrots, celery, cucumbers, eggplant, lettuce, peppers, Swiss chard, and watermelon— but they warn that the oil could burn the tender leaves of plants like squash, cauliflower, and red cabbage. Be sure to wash your vegetables well at harvest to remove any residues (eating soap can really upset your stomach).

Neem extract also kills whiteflies. This botanical insecticide has a long history in India but is a relatively recent player here in the New World. It's available under various brand names and seems to be harmless to children, pets, birds, and so on. When insects eat foliage sprayed with neem, they become too sick to continue eating. Use it sparingly, though, because neem is also toxic to beneficial insects.

Or you can mix up a garlic spray, which is also effective against whiteflies. Just puree a couple cloves of garlic with a pint of water in a blender, strain, and spray.

A number of tiny wasps parasitize whiteflies, and lacewings and ladybugs will eat whiteflies. That's one reason you shouldn't use toxic insecticides in your garden—they kill those good insects as well (and often much more effectively) as the bad. If you want to go the beneficial route, grow lots of flowers and herbs (let the herbs flower); such plants will provide a continuous supply of pollen and nectar that will attract those whitefly-hungry beneficials.

The Beneficial Insect Company in Fort Mill, South Carolina, is one company that sells whitefly sticky traps (see "Resources" on page 234). Or you can make your own traps. First, cut rectangular pieces of some thin, firm material such as plastic or durable cardboard. Drill a hole at one side (for hanging), or glue two together with a stick between them (for sticking into the soil). Paint the surface of the rectangles a bright lemon yellow, the color that attracts whiteflies. When the paint is dry, coat the pieces with an insect-trapping adhesive such as Tanglefoot, which you should be able to find in any garden-supply store. Position the traps—the more the better—around your garden a few inches above the plants.

Invasion of the Grasshoppers

Q: *For 4 years now we've been invaded by grasshoppers—all kinds. My flowers are becoming sticks. We didn't even have to mow the grass! What's the reason for all the grasshoppers and what can we do about them?*

A: Your town is probably surrounded by wheat fields, guesses Leroy Brooks, extension entomologist at Kansas State University. Grainfields are prime grasshopper territory, and grasshoppers like to lay their eggs in weedy, uncultivated areas. If your property is in fallow land that's surrounded by grainfields, you may have quite a battle on your hands.

Brooks suggests searching out and disturbing favorite hatching sites such as weedy fencerows or ditch banks in both spring and fall to kill grasshopper eggs laid in that soil. If your property is surrounded by large uncultivated areas, you might heed the warning of Whitney Cranshaw, Ph.D., extension entomologist at Colorado State University, who says "don't mow. People who mow down all the weedy areas around their land make their garden an oasis for grasshoppers. Leave some lush green growth nearby so the grasshoppers have a place to feast besides your garden."

You can also try managing them with a microbial control called *Nosema locustae.* This naturally occurring pathogen sickens young grasshoppers and crickets after they eat it but doesn't harm mammals, fish, or even other insects. To be effective, you should apply it shortly after the eggs hatch, where breeding hoppers are developing. It's available in garden centers and farm-supply stores under such brand names as Grasshopper Attack, Grasshopper Control, Nolo Bait, and Semaspore.

You could also get your feathered friends to lend a hand by providing them with some water sources and nesting boxes. *Many* kinds of birds are voracious grasshopper eaters, including bluebirds, crows, flycatchers, kingbirds, horned larks, and grasshopper sparrows. And guinea hens are reputed to be even more effective at controlling grasshoppers than chickens are.

Floating row covers can offer some protection as well. "Bear in mind that grasshopper infestations are cyclical; they're usually severe only for 2 or 3 years," says Dr. Cranshaw. Maybe you're due for a respite.

No More Mosquitoes

Q: *I enjoy growing water lilies in pans of water, but my pans seem to breed mosquitoes no matter how often I change the water. Is there something I can put in the water that will discourage the insects without killing my flowers?*

A: You can use *Bacillus thuringiensis* var. *israelensis* (BTI), a naturally occurring bacteria that is the active ingredient in a product called Mosquito Dunks. The dunks float in still water (where mosquitoes prefer to breed) and release the BTI, which is toxic to mosquito larvae but will not harm your plants or you. BTI is also available as a liquid spray product called Vectobac for treating large areas of mosquito or blackfly habitat. If your community routinely sprays toxic chemical insecticides to control these insects, tell your pest-control officials about this nontoxic alternative.

Like Moths to a Cabbage

Q: *I have white moths eating my broccoli, cauliflower, and cabbage. Someone told me that interplanting marigolds with the veggies would keep the moths away. Is that true?*

A: Those white moths (imported cabbageworm adults) aren't eating your crops—they're laying eggs on the leaves. The wormlike caterpillars that hatch are most likely the culprits that are doing the damage.

Trials conducted in California found that growing cabbage amid marigold plants slightly reduced the numbers of larvae, but not their damage. Growing one plant of cabbage amid four of anise (*Pimpinella anisum*) significantly reduced the number of imported cabbageworm eggs. However, the cabbage didn't do all that well and yields were reduced. And while marigolds don't seem to repel the moths, planting almost any flowering plant near your garden is a good way to attract beneficial insects that will take care of these and other pest insects. Several years ago at the Rodale Institute Experimental Farm in Maxatawny, Pennsylvania, entomologist Diane Matthews-Gehringer found that lemon gem marigolds (those dainty marigolds with small, single, edible flowers) attract spiders and lots of parasitic miniwasps.

Spiders eat all kinds of insects and insect eggs. Parasitic wasps will parasitize your cabbage pest's eggs or larvae by laying their own eggs inside them. To attract even more wasps (they feed on small flowers with easily accessible nectar and pollen), be sure to plant some herbs with flat, umbrella-shaped flowers, such as dill and fennel, and let some Queen-Anne's-lace grow nearby. Yes, even weeds can add to the biological diversity of your garden—flowering dandelions provide early meals of pollen for ladybugs, which also eat imported cabbageworm eggs.

Nasty Nematodes

Q: *I have a real problem with nematodes. They have completely destroyed my cole crops—broccoli, cabbage, cauliflower, and brussels sprouts—for the past 5 years. I've tried many cures but have found none to be effective, and I would appreciate any help or suggestions you can give.*

A: Yes, nematodes *can* be a real problem. Some members of this large family of tiny soil-dwelling creatures tunnel into the roots of plants, impairing the plants' ability to take up water and nutrients, and opening up those plants to fungal and bacterial infections.

Before you can take any action, you have to find out exactly what kind of nematode is in your soil. Contact your county extension office; the agent there will ask you to send in a soil or root sample, which will be tested for nematodes. There are 50 to 60 different species, and you need to know exactly which one you're dealing with before you can choose the most effective remedy. Controls usually involve some combination of rotating crops, using a cover crop, or growing plants that nematodes wouldn't touch with a 10-foot pole.

You see, different nematodes feed on different plants. If you don't grow the types of plants that your specific variety needs to eat, they will gradually die off. For example, root-knot nematodes feed on lettuce, onions, tomatoes, and okra, but they won't eat corn, wheat, and other grains. So if you only grow plants they can't eat for a couple years in your nematode-infected soil, you'll make it hard—perhaps impossible—for those nematodes to be fruitful and multiply.

And if you grow a cover crop that your nematodes *really* don't like, you can drive the little beasties out *much* faster. Some cover crops—including brassicas like rapeseed, mustard or oil radishes, and sudangrass—release compounds that are very toxic to root-knot nematodes, says George Abawi, Ph.D., professor of plant pathology at Cornell University. Unfortunately, it sounds like *your* particular nematodes would just love those brassica covers. So again, identify your *specific* pest. Your extension agent should then be able to suggest vegetable varieties that are *resistant* to those nematodes. 'Better Boy' tomato, for instance, is very resistant to the common root-knot nematode, says Dr. Abawi.

There's also a drastic "clean fallow" option. This involves removing *all* plants and roots from your garden for a full year (so the nematodes have *nothing* to eat) and cultivating the soil frequently during the hottest part of the summer to expose those hungry nematodes to the sun. Then you could plant whatever you wanted the next season.

A few last tips from Dr. Abawi: Be sure that your soil is as healthy as possible. Nematodes are present everywhere, but plants growing in very rich soils high in organic matter can withstand more nematode stress. In fact, he says that the very presence of high levels of organic matter is suppressive to nematodes. And don't forget marigolds; they really do deter nematodes. The ones with the most pungent foliage work the best, says Ian Merwin, Ph.D., Cornell pomologist, who has used cover crops of 'Sparky' French marigolds to suppress root lesion nematode, a very common garden and orchard pest. Grow the marigolds for a season, plow them under, and then plant whatever you like the following year.

Rose Woes

Q: *I'm having trouble with a thing called a rose midge. I have a half dozen rosebushes of various types in my garden, but for the past two summers I have enjoyed very few roses. I want to be organic; what can I do?*

A: The rose midge is a tiny insect that lays its eggs in the growing points—the buds and branch tips—of rosebushes. The eggs hatch into tiny larvae that feed on these tender parts. Afflicted buds become black, undersized, and crooked. If you take a hand lens and probe with a tweezers, you'll find tiny little whitish larvae less than ⅛ inch long.

Stephen Scanniello, rosarian for 5,000 rosebushes at the Cranford Rose Garden at the Brooklyn Botanic Garden, says "the best thing to do is to prune off the afflicted areas and destroy them—*don't* compost them." And prune severely—don't leave too much wood behind, he adds.

The larvae don't stay on the foliage very long before they drop down into the soil to pupate. Eventually they emerge from the soil as small flying insects, and the cycle continues. So inspect your roses daily, and if you find signs of midge damage, use those pruners.

Squashing Sowbugs

Q: *All the garden pests I have are tolerable except sowbugs. These monsters thrive in the compost (yes, it is hot, and I turn it frequently), and at night I can see hundreds of them in my garden defoliating beans, skinning squash, and clear-cutting seedlings. They even gang up on my drought-tolerant, tough-skinned native plants. What can I do? How about chickens?*

A: Chickens would probably eat some of these creatures, but they'd have to scratch them out of wherever they're hiding during the day—and as you've noted, sowbugs (and pillbugs) are nocturnal. Some experts believe that "sowbugs get blamed for more damage than they actually do . . . because they are frequently found in decaying fruit . . . damaged by other pests such as snails and slugs." (That quote was from University of California IPM experts writing in *Pests of the Garden and Small Farm,* University of California, 1990.)

Large numbers of sowbugs can cause severe damage to seedlings and vegetables lying on the soil, but they mostly feed on decaying organic material. "They are also quite important in soil ecosystems," says Clay Sassaman, Ph.D, chair of the University of California at Riverside's biology department. "They change dead vegetation into humus, making the nutrients in that dead vegetation available to plants." (That's why they're so at home in your compost pile; it's what they do.)

Sowbugs and pillbugs are crustaceans. They breathe through modified gills and need a moist environment. Only in very moist conditions can they become "very abundant and cause such problems in a garden," says Dr. Sassaman, who advises you to "keep all litter away from the base of your plants, don't overwater, and don't mulch any more than necessary." (If you must mulch, use materials that are coarse enough to let water pass through easily.)

Are you using an overhead sprinkler system? Drip irrigation would be better because the surface of your garden would stay drier. Whichever system you use, try to water early in the day so the soil surface dries out before evening. Trellis whatever crops you can, such as cucumbers, melons, and squash; remove old decaying leaves; and clean up any place (piles of flowerpots, boards, other garden materials, etc.) where these critters could seek cover during the day.

Trash Thrips; Vanquish Virus

Q: *For the last two years I've had a problem with tomato spotted wilt virus. Our Canadian equivalent of an extension agent has simply advised me to destroy the plants. Is there an organic control?*

A: Before you can control tomato spotted wilt virus, you have to control western flower thrips, the tiny (less than 1/20 inch long), sucking insects that spread the virus from plant to plant, says Bob Martin, Ph.D., research scientist with Agriculture Canada in Vancouver.

Western flower thrips are very common and widespread. One of the easiest ways to keep them off your tomatoes is to simply shroud your plants with floating row covers. Drape it over your plants' supports (stakes, cages, etc.) as soon as you set the plants out in the garden, and be sure you have enough material to cover late lush growth.

Getting rid of weeds before they flower will also mean fewer thrips, adds David Gillespie, Ph.D., research scientist at Agriculture Canada's Agassiz Research Station in British Columbia. "*Anything* flowering will attract western flower thrips," he warns, "especially clover."

Other controls include sticky traps (long, narrow, yellow panels coated with a sticky substance and hung vertically, protruding partially above the crop) and insecticidal soap sprays. Maintain a *very* vigorous soil containing lots of organic matter, and you'll create an inviting environment for the predators (ground beetles, rove beetles, and predatory mites) that feed on thrips pupae, which develop in the soil. Frequent, shallow cultivation around your garden plants will help destroy those pupae as well.

Thrips often migrate into gardens from cut hay fields. If your garden is next to one of these, protect it with a hedgerow-type planting that breaks the wind. That windbreaker will also provide a haven for tiny parasitic wasps, another beneficial insect that preys on thrips, says Dr. Gillespie.

And, yes, you *should* get rid of plants infected by the virus promptly; *you* can spread the disease while pruning or picking if you leave debris in place. The symptoms, which you know all too well (but we include here for those who don't), are general decline of the plant, big dark brown or black lesions on the leaves, and/or off-color lesions with brown or black halos on the fruit itself. Burn or trash the plants; don't just leave them near your garden, and don't compost them, says Dr. Martin. The virus is not soilborne, but if you leave diseased plants around your garden, thrips can spread the disease to healthy plants.

Discouraging Ticks

Q: *My family and I are moving to a farm. Besides clearing the brush, what steps can I take to best reduce the tick population?*

A: Clearing brush is one of the most important tactics in the battle against ticks. They *need* brush or tall grass to crawl up on to drop onto their hosts. Remove as much of this kind of hip-high vegetation as possible, says Darryl Sanders, Ph.D., extension urban entomologist at the University of Missouri. "Create a little island around the house and yard. If you put in grass, make sure you keep it well mowed for some distance beyond the limits of human and pet activity," he says.

In their detailed report "Managing Ticks, the Least-Toxic Way," William Olkowski, Helga Olkowski, and Sheila Daar of the Bio-Integral Resource Center point out that ticks prefer humid environments, so trim your tree branches so sunlight can reach the ground to dry it out, they advise. And if you must water your lawn, do it deeply but *infrequently*—so it can dry out thoroughly between waterings.

Ticks feed on birds and white-tailed deer before moving on to people and dogs, so *don't* feed these creatures on your property. All it takes is a couple of pregnant female ticks falling off a bird or a deer to send the local tick population soaring.

Pennies from Heaven

Q: *We have hard well water and insecticidal soap is not very effective when mixed with it. Is there some inexpensive solution? We have serious aphid problems this year due to a mild winter.*

A: The agents at the extension office in Lehigh County, Pennsylvania, came up with an ingenious solution to the hard water/insecticidal soap problem: rainwater. The next time it pours, set out a clean bucket or basin. The stuff you collect from the sky should have a pH that's just about neutral. Pour it into containers with lids, and store a bunch so you'll always have a supply on hand.

CHECK IT OUT!

With Lyme disease becoming so widespread, discovering a tick on your body can be an unsettling experience. Here's a way you can turn the tables on ticks—add guinea fowl to your arsenal. Guineas are about the same size as chickens with faces only a mother could love. Farmers and homeowners have been using them for years to keep infestations under control. The birds require little care and can roost outside during the summer.

Oil Can Be Easy on Beneficials

Q: *The application of "dormant oil" is usually suggested as a means of controlling various insects and pests such as mites. How "selective" is this type of pest control? Are predatory mites and other beneficial insects also at risk of being affected by this treatment?*

A: "Dormant oil" is a horticultural grade of oil sprayed on trees in their dormant stage (hence the name)—usually the trees are sprayed in late winter or early spring, before they start growing for the season. At this time of the year, notorious pests like European red mites and San Jose scale are in their immature stage and are particularly vulnerable to the oil, which coats and suffocates them.

But "most beneficial mites and insects will *not* be affected by the oil spray because they won't come in contact with it," assures Larry Hull, Ph.D., professor of entomology at the Penn State Fruit Research and Extension Center in Biglerville, Pennsylvania. "In late winter and early spring, when the oil is applied, beneficials aren't on the surfaces of trees—they're overwintering in the groundcover beneath the tree or are hidden beneath its bark."

Even "summer oils," horticultural oils that are lighter (because they're much more highly refined) so that you can safely spray them on growing trees without damaging them, have little effect on beneficials, comments Dr. Hull. "Like dormant oil, summer oil is basically used to suffocate the *egg stage* of pests, but most beneficials live outside the orchard and don't move in until the pests begin to build up. The best time to spray fruit trees with summer oil to control spider mites (especially European red mites) is 1 to 2 weeks after the flower petals fall off. That's when the fewest beneficials are going to be found on the trees," he explains.

You can even use ultralight insecticidal oils in the vegetable garden without harming too many good bugs. Unfortunately, soft-bodied insects like lacewings and beneficials in their larval stage will probably die if they get sprayed with the oil, but it wouldn't be particularly harmful to hard-shelled beneficials like adult ladybugs. Also, "parasites that are pupating inside their insect hosts are probably not going to be affected, and any predators and parasites that fly in after the application will be affected even less," says Mary Louise Flint, Ph.D., entomologist with the University of California at Davis and coauthor of the manual, *Managing Insects and Mites with Spray Oil* (University of California Division of Agriculture and Natural Resources, 1991).

To protect beneficials, limit spraying to small areas where you *know* pests are lurking and leave some unsprayed refugees within your garden for the good guys. Spray early in the morning before bees become active, *don't* spray during peak flowering times—to protect beneficials that feed on nectar—and don't spray on flowers. And, of course, "if you have plans to release beneficials, wait until after the oil application to do so," says Dr. Flint.

CONTROLLING CRITTERS

Animal Kingdom

Q: *I'm 75 years old and have gardened all my life. I live right on Main Street at the edge of town, but moose, deer, raccoons, squirrels, and rabbits still plague my garden—even though it's surrounded by a fence. The only thing that seems to keep these critters out of my growables is hanging a man's dirty work clothes in the garden—but on Main Street?!? Would an*

ultrasonic pest-repelling devico work? My next alternative is an electric fence.

A: Those ultrasonic devices are iffy, at best. "They may work for a short time, but eventually animals get used to them, and they stop working. It's like living in a noisy apartment—sooner or later you just don't really hear the noise any more," explains Bill Quarles, Ph.D., managing editor of the *IPM Practitioner*, the publication of the Bio-Integral Resource Center in Berkeley, California, an organization dedicated to finding the least toxic ways to control all kinds of pests.

And ultrasonic probably wouldn't work at all against those deer and moose, adds George Laidlaw, senior coordination officer with Health Canada's Pest Management Regulatory Agency, who explains that companies must prove their pest-control devices actually work before they can sell them in Canada. Laidlaw says that regular old "sonic" devices—contraptions that emit loud, blaring, and irritating noises—can be effective against deer, but then you're back to the possibility of offending your neighbors.

The electric fencing you're considering will keep many kinds of animals out of a garden. And you can even buy what you need locally—one of New England's oldest fence dealers sells a kit system that should keep out your moose, deer, rabbits, and raccoons. It's an electrified dark green netting strung on black posts that's attractive enough to be the envy of your Main Street neighbors. For more information, write to Wellscroft Farm Fence Systems, 167 Sunset Hill, Chesham, Harrisville, NH 03450.

However, one animal that will not be stopped by fencing of any kind is the squirrel. To exclude these furry little acrobats, you must figure out what's drawing them to your garden in the first place. Squirrels are attracted to different foods than rabbits, raccoons, and deer, explains Dr. Quarles. Specifically, they eat lots of nuts and seeds. So if possible, locate your garden away from bird feeders (squirrels love birdseed) and nut trees, advises Russell Libby, executive director of the Maine Organic Farmers and Gardeners Association. Or lure the squirrels to a different area by feeding them something inexpensive, like field corn, suggests Libby.

Pecan-Loving Pests

Q: *We have two lovely pecan trees, and they have done well this year, but is there anything we can do about the squirrels, crows, and blue jays that carry away and eat pounds of nuts?*

A: If your trees are isolated, that is, more than squirrel-jumping distance from other trees and buildings, you may be able to keep these arboreal rodents away from your pecans by encasing the tree trunks in some kind of light, unclimbable metal. Specifically, try a 3-foot band of smooth metal around the trunk, beginning 3 to 8 feet above the ground. Be sure to trim any low branches so squirrels can't get a leg up.

When it comes to birds, wildlife experts agree on only one thing: Try lots of different deterrents, be persistent, and change tactics frequently to keep the birds on edge (and away from your trees). Your bird-spooking rotation should include scarecrows, scare eyes, fake snakes, shiny plastic streamers, noisemakers, and loud music (put an old radio out there and fiddle with the dial until you find a station they don't like).

Get a dog or invite friends that have one to bring their pooch for a visit. You can also erect a few 10- to 20-foot poles topped with small crossbars around your area as roosting places for owls and hawks, a small mammal control technique recommended by R. L. Carlton, a wildlife biologist, in the book *Nut Tree Culture in North America*, published by the Northern Nut Growers Association.

And don't forget to harvest promptly. Pecans are ripe when they fall to the ground or you can shake them from the tree.

Chicken wire is another

old-time solution to

keeping cats out of your

garden, or even away from

your birdbath. Just unroll

some chicken wire and

spread it out flat around

the outside of the beds.

Even though the freshly

tilled soil (or delicious little

birds!) may look tempting

to your feline friends, they

won't walk on the coarse

wire to get to them. When

the cats have learned to

stay away, you can take up

the chicken wire and

replace it with mulch.

Grapes in the Bag

Q: *I have a dozen grapevines, and each year I lose at least half the crop to birds. In his book* **From Vines to Wines** *(Storey Communications, 1985), Jeff Cox recommends bagging the grape clusters and identifies a company that manufactures waterproof white parchment bags, but I was unable to reach the company at the address given. Is there another source for these bags? Do you really need special bags?*

A: Lon Rombough, grape consultant for the North American Fruit Explorers, says that "unless you live in an area with a lot of summer rainfall, regular old brown or white paper bags are all you'll need. I use them and have left them on so long that they look like lace, but they still keep the birds out."

When you bag the grape clusters, "always position the bag with the seam side toward the ground," suggests Rombough. This will help keep the bag together longer. He cautions that if you leave the bags on for a long time, paper wasps might chew them and earwigs might nest in them, but neither pest "seems to hurt the fruit."

For those of you without Jeff Cox's book handy, here's how to bag grapes: Cut off both bottom corners of the bag so water can drain out. Slit the sides of the bag a couple inches down from the open end at both sides, then slide a half-grown cluster into the bag, gather the top of the bag around the vine and tape it shut.

Keeping Out Kitty

Q: *How can I keep our cats from using the garden as a litter box?*

A: Keep cats out of the garden using a combination of fences, repellents, or mulches. If a long dry spell follows seed sowing, turn on a sprinkler to dampen the soil. Not only will this help seeds, but wet soil is less attractive to cats. Lay twigs across the soil, or use cardboard or plastic mulch to prevent your pets from digging. Try planting clumps of alliums, chamomile, marigolds, and rue, which are believed to repel cats. You also may want to plant a patch of catnip at the edge or even further from your garden to draw cats' interest away.

If they do get through your defenses, remove feces along with the soil immediately surrounding it. More than 40 percent of cats in the United States carry the parasite *Toxoplasma gondii*. The parasite is excreted in their feces and if contracted by pregnant women, can cause brain disease and impaired vision or blindness in the unborn child. Young children and adults with weak immune systems also are at risk. *T. gondii* can remain infective in cat feces outdoors for 12 to 18 months.

Gardeners are more likely to pick up the parasite directly on their hands than from the vegetables grown in the garden. Scrub and peel root vegetables, and boil produce if you still have doubts. Thoroughly wash your hands, and wear gloves when gardening if your cats continue to use your garden as a litter box.

Slithering Serpents

Q: *How can we get rid of snakes? We know they eat bugs, but our property is overrun with them.*

A: If your snakes aren't poisonous, why not try to live with them? They're quiet, pretty, and best of all, they eat caterpillars, grasshoppers, and many other insects. Larger snakes even eat small rodents, including pocket gophers, house mice, meadow mice, voles, and brown rats.

The majority of the snakes you might encounter in the East or Midwest are garter snakes, king snakes, or black snakes,

and these are very beneficial, says Douglas Taylor, Ph.D., zo-
ology professor at Miami University in Ohio and treasurer of
the Society for the Study of Amphibians and Reptiles.

Excessive numbers of any animal suggests that there is
plenty of food and habitat for them, Dr. Taylor says. If you
truly have a snake problem, you can try to reduce their numbers by removing their favored shelters: piles of logs, brush,
trash, building materials, rocks, and so on. (Snakes don't
hang out in gardens or open, grassy areas.) But be aware
that their presence is an indicator that your property might
well have a large population of insects or rodents, their
favorite foods, which they are currently keeping under control for you.

Vamoose, Voles

Q: *Our community garden was literally overrun with
voles this past summer. They were even scooting
around the paths while we worked in our plots. They did
quite a number on our bean and pea plants. We're trying
to keep debris and any sort of vole cover to a minimum,
but the little devils are so small they can nest under a
lettuce leaf. Hardware-cloth fencing around our plots
was suggested but would be difficult and scratchy to
reach over. Any ideas for controlling the little critters?*

A: Voles are small rodents, slightly larger than mice, but
with smaller ears that are positioned close to their heads
and tails that are much shorter. By the time you notice
damage from voles, you probably have a large population on
your hands. Voles are prolific breeders averaging three to
four litters per year, with each litter containing four to seven
volettes. And a well-tended organic garden—with its deep,
loose soil, lush mulches, and delicious edibles—is the perfect place to raise a vole family.

"The best time to control voles is in the early spring or fall," suggests Paul Curtis, Ph.D., an extension associate at Cornell University. And the only effective control is to trap them, he says. You can use snap traps that are normally used to kill mice, or you can use a live trap. (Dr. Curtis recommends the 2 × 2½ × 6½-inch Sherman live traps available directly from H. B. Sherman Traps, Inc. (see "Resources" on page 234).

It is very important that you place any trap correctly. Identify the "runways" that the voles are currently using by looking for pieces of the crops they've been feeding on inside their little tunnels. Dig out a small area in front of each tunnel, set a trap in the excavated area, and because voles like to be under cover, cover it with a piece of wood or cardboard, advises Dr. Curtis. Bait your traps with apple chunks, which the little critters find irresistible. If you use live traps, release the voles in a wooded area, far far away from your garden.

Or turn the tables and put the little munchers on the menu! "Everything eats them," says Richard Chipman, wildlife biologist for the USDA animal damage control unit in Montpelier, Vermont. Predators such as snakes, cats, hawks, and owls will all help to keep vole numbers down if you eliminate hiding places like brush piles and mulches and keep the grass cut short so predators can spot them easily.

In areas where birds of prey live or migrate, you can encourage them to feast on your voles by erecting perches for the birds. Washington State University's Leonard Askham, Ph.D., recommends placing a perch at each of the four corners of your garden. "They don't have to be overly tall, but they should have cross bars in *both* directions so the birds can perch in any wind direction," he suggests. If any old, dead trees are nearby, leave them be—they make ideal perches for pest eaters.

You can also create and erect nesting boxes to attract raptors like hawks and owls. To purchase a copy of Dr. Askham's bulletin on this subject, which includes plans for owl and kestrel boxes, contact the Bulletins Office, Washington State University, Cooper Publications Building, Dept. WB, P.O. Box 645912, Pullman, WA 99164-5912, and ask about Publication #EB1602.

Bulb-Chomping Rodents

Q: *How can I stop voles from nibbling on my tulips all winter and rabbits and squirrels from munching on the new growth in spring?*

A: Unfortunately, voles, squirrels, and rabbits can't resist munching on tulips—they just taste too good. In fact, bulb lovers beware: Voles, mice, squirrels, and rabbits will dine on crocuses, hyacinths, lilies, and blue grape hyacinths as well.

To thwart voles' botanical cravings, try throwing a handful of sharp, crushed gravel (about the size of peas) into the hole when planting tulips in fall. Strategic plantings of foul-smelling crown imperial fritillaria among tulips may help repel rodents, too. Although you can try to repel the squirrels and rabbits with bloodmeal, human hair, or ground-up peppers in a soapy solution, the best control is an underground physical barrier. Baskets made from mesh hardware cloth work well, but use your imagination (and materials on hand).

You can also experiment with different varieties of bulbs in the hope of finding one whose flavor the critters don't care for much. In informal observations at the Brooklyn Botanic Garden (favorite dining spot of a large number of furry connoisseurs), horticulturists found that within the crocuses, *C. biflorus* 'Fairy' and *C. tomasinianus*, including 'Whitewell Purple', escaped squirrel consumption.

And if all this sounds like more work than you're up for, you can plant bulbs other than tulips. Scillas, daffodils, and endymion are "less-preferred" meals, as are allium, chionodoxa, colchicum, and galanthus.

Deer- and Beetle-Proof Your Plants

Q: *Can you please compile a list of ornamentals and evergreens that aren't bothered by either deer or Japanese beetles?*

A: The plants that *both* of your banes have been known to avoid, according to lists compiled by Bill Quarles, Ph.D., of the Bio-Integral Resource Center (deer) and David Shetlar, Ph.D., landscape entomologist at Ohio State University (beetles) are: columbine, dogwood, firs, foxglove, hemlock, hollies, lilacs, magnolias, and pines. (Just remember that when food is scarce, hungry creatures will chow down on anything.)

Specifically *deer*-proof plants (per Dr. Quarles) include aloe, baby's tears, black bamboo, weeping birch, boxwood, bridal wreath, sea buckthorn, butterfly bush, cedar, century plant, chinaberry tree, clematis, crocus, ferns, golden-bells, hercules club, hyacinths, iris, ixia, jasmine, larkspur, lily-of-the-valley, black locust, mock orange, mountain laurel, muscari, narcissus, pepper tree, persimmon, shadbush, smoke tree, sparaxis, snowball viburnum, and wax myrtle; aromatic plants like rosemary, lavender, thyme, and some salvias; and garlic and onions, too.

Japanese beetle–safe selections (named by Dr. Shetlar) include ageratum, arborvitae, ash, baby's breath, garden balsam, begonia, bleeding heart, boxwood, buttercups, caladium, carnations, Chinese lantern plant, cockscomb, coral-bells, coralberry, coreopsis, cornflower, daisies, dusty miller, euonymus, false cypresses, forget-me-not, forsythia, hydrangeas, junipers, ornamental kale, lilies, red or silver maples, mulberry, nasturtium, red and white oaks, poppies, snapdragon, snowberry, speedwell, sweet pea, sweet William, tulip trees, violets, pansies, and yews.

Chapter

8

WEEDS

In the gardening world, the word "weed" is practically synonymous with "problem." After all, you'd never wish for creeping Charlie, dodder, or kudzu to take over your garden or landscape. But that doesn't mean you need to reach for the herbicides—you *can* control weeds organically. Here's how.

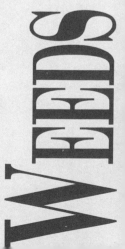

GENERAL INFORMATION

Organic Weed Control

Q: *Help! I'm a novice gardener who just moved to a country acreage with a huge, neglected garden that's overrun with weeds. What's the best way to clear this weed patch safely, without using any chemicals?*

A: It will probably take a full year or two to bring such a weedy area under control because even after you kill off all the visible weeds, there will still be lots of seeds in the soil that will be ready to sprout at the first opportunity. The first thing you need to do is rototill or plow the area. Then water the tilled soil to encourage seeds near the surface to sprout. Wait 2 to 4 weeks, then rake out any perennial weed roots that have sprouted and cultivate again, shallowly. This two-step tilling process will reduce the number of weeds that will sprout to compete with your crops. Plant your crops as soon as possible after you complete the second tilling.

Lay out your beds or rows so that you can easily mulch or mow between them. If you have time before you plant, bring in a load of blended compost and soil from a garden center, and spread it at least a couple of inches deep over the planting areas. You'll bury any weed seeds that were brought to the surface during the second tilling, and you'll improve the soil.

Now, buy a good weeding hoe, such as a stirrup or diamond hoe. Use it early and often, cultivating shallowly to kill any sprouted weeds without stirring up the remaining buried weed seeds. Once your soil is warm and crops are up, mulch as much of the garden as possible with straw or grass clippings. To smother weeds and build the soil in all unplanted areas, plant cover crops, such as buckwheat (in summer) and rye (in fall).

Don't be discouraged if you still have lots of weeds the first season. Reclaiming a weedy, neglected area, such as yours, is one of the biggest challenges a gardener can face.

When Is a Soap an Herbicide?

Q: *Both Safer's Insecticidal Soap and Safer Superfast Weed & Grass Killer herbicide list "potassium salts of fatty acids" as the active ingredient on their labels. Is it just a higher concentration of this ingredient that kills weeds?*

A: Although the ingredient label for both products says "potassium salts of fatty acids," they aren't exactly the same thing. All soaps are made by mixing fats or oils with an alkali such as lye or a similar substance. By chemical reaction, the mineral in the alkali forms a salt with the fat. This process is called saponification and results in the soaps that we are familiar with.

Insecticidal soap is made using unsaturated long-chain fatty acids (such as oleic acid) from animal fats. These long-chain fatty acids dissolve insect skin or cuticle while preserving the protective cuticle of most plants. Herbicidal soap is made from shorter-chain fatty acids from vegetable sources—mostly coconut and palm oils— and these plant-based fats are extremely effective at disrupting plant cells.

Is Roundup Safe?

Q: *Can you please tell me how harmful, beneficial, or benign to the environment the herbicide product Roundup is? The ads you see in newspapers and on TV make it sound like it's as safe as water, but I can't find objective information about its effects.*

A: Although those massive ad campaigns make Roundup seem as harmless as water, the truth is that it's a pretty nasty chemical herbicide. To begin with, Roundup is toxic to earthworms, fish, and a number of beneficial insects including parasitic wasps, lacewings, ladybugs, and predatory mites, explains Caroline Cox, editor of the excellent *Journal of Pesticide Reform*, published by the Northwest Coalition for Alternatives to Pesticides (NCAP).

Roundup's active ingredient, glyphosate, affects plants and animals in other ways, too, cites Cox: Research conducted by T. B. Moorman and colleagues at the USDA Southern Weed Science Laboratory in Stoneville, Mississippi, found that glyphosate reduces soybeans' and clover's ability to fix nitrogen; a study conducted by G. S. Johal and J. E. Rahe of the Center for Pest Management at Simon Fraser University in Burnaby, British Columbia, found that glyphosate makes bean plants more susceptible to disease; and at Dalhousie University in Halifax, Nova Scotia, D. Estok and colleagues found that glyphosate reduces the growth of beneficial soil-dwelling mycorrhizal fungi.

Moving up to mammals, sperm production in rabbits was cut 50 percent when they were exposed to glyphosate in research conducted by M. I. Yousef and colleagues at the University of Alexandria in Egypt and the University of Tromso in Norway. And the effects of glyphosate on humans are no bargain either. In California, where pesticide-related illness must be reported, Roundup's active ingredient was the third most commonly reported cause of pesticide illness among agricultural workers and the most common cause of pesticide illness in landscape workers. According to two New Zealand toxicologists, the symptoms experienced by workers exposed to Roundup included eye and skin irritation, headaches, nausea, and heart palpitations.

On top of all this, Roundup can linger in the soil for a long time under some conditions, says Cox. In a study conducted by Monsanto (Roundup's manufacturer), lettuce, carrots, and barley were planted in soil where Roundup had been used a year earlier, and "when they harvested those crops, Roundup was detected in them," reports Cox.

Want more? Cox has written a fact sheet on glyphosate—contact NCAP, P.O. Box 1393, Eugene, OR 97440; (541) 344-5044; fax (541) 344-6923; Web site: www.pesticide.org; e-mail: infor@pesticide.org.

SPECIFIC WEED WOES

Bye Bye Bermudagrass

Q: *How can we control the spread of bermudagrass organically? I pulled it all out of one part of the yard by hand but made the mistake of putting it on a composting weed pile. Now I'm faced with a larger patch than I started with.*

A: Bermudagrass spreads both aboveground (with stolons) and below (with roots), says Jim Brooks, director of the Lawn Institute, a turfgrass information center. He adds that simply pulling or digging it out is one of the best ways to get rid of small amounts but that power equipment can be a big help with a patch that's too big for such a personal touch. He suggests you use a tiller to dig up the area in fall, "tilling deeply—4 to 6 inches deep—to get at all of the root system, then rake up all the roots, and dispose of them someplace where they won't take hold again."

A lazier way to make bermudagrass go away is to spray it with an organic (soap-based) herbicide like Safer Superfast Weed & Grass Killer. Just be aware that you'll have to spray two or three times—possibly even more depending on how deeply it is rooted—to starve out the roots. Superfast is available at garden and home centers.

In a Bind

Q: *A morning glory-type weed has infested our garden, and pulling it out by hand hasn't worked. Please offer a nonherbicidal solution soon, or I could be taken prisoner.*

A: Your weed is most probably field bindweed (*Convolvulus arvensis*), a creeping, climbing invader from Europe that's also known as small-flowered morning glory, cornbine, creeping Jenny, and—particularly apropos—devil's guts. It's indeed devilishly difficult to do in. In a single season, one plant can grow roots that spread over a 10-foot circle and reach down deep; up to 25 daughter plants may sprout from the connected root system. When you remove only the aboveground growth, the plant draws on food stored in its huge remaining root system to send up new shoots—again and again. Even chemical herbicides can't easily defeat this green devil.

To eradicate bindweed, you must be very persistent. Pull or hoe it all as soon as you spot any new growth. Watch for it to sneak into bushes or up plant stems. You can smother dense patches with heavy carpeting or cardboard, but you'll still constantly need to watch for and remove any plants that sprout around the edges. Never till bindweed unless you're prepared to keep tilling every 10 days for one or two full seasons. (Tilling less often just breaks up and spreads the roots around; then they sprout even more plants.) If the infestation is really severe, you might need to move your garden to a new site until you can eradicate the bindweed.

Killing Comfrey

Q: *Comfrey is taking over my garden. I spend hours digging up the roots but I can't seem to get rid of it. What can I do?*

A: Don't despair. All that digging has probably weakened the plants enough that you're now ready for step two, explains Conrad Richter, vice president of Richter's Herb Nursery in Goodwood, Ontario. First, make sure you've removed the biggest roots and cut the leaves off the remaining plants (add the leaves to your compost pile), then cover your comfrey-choked areas with black plastic, carpet, or some other impenetrable material. Weigh this barrier down with a heavy layer of soil or a thick mulch to keep any little roots that have been left behind from sprouting. Keep the area covered for at least 1 year and your problem should be smothered.

Curbing Creeping Charlie

Q: *Can you help me eradicate, or at least seriously intimidate, the pernicious weed Glechoma hederacea, commonly known as ground ivy, gill-over-the-ground, and creeping Charlie? I've been pulling it up by the bushel and smothering it with newspaper, black plastic, and/or wet grass trimmings, but nothing contains it. Don't tell me it makes a great groundcover; please tell me how to get rid of it.*

A: We talked to a host of horticulturists, and none held out much hope of getting rid of your pest, even if you were to turn to heavy-duty chemical herbicides (which, of course, you wouldn't). Then we heard about the work of a former Iowa State University graduate student, Harleen Hatterman-Valenti, Ph.D.

Dr. Hatterman-Valenti, now a research biologist with FMC Corporation in New Jersey, discovered that you could kill ground ivy in turfgrass by spraying it with a solution of borax and water. Before you try this, however, you need to know a few things.

Borax, or more specifically its active ingredient, boron, can be toxic to plants. Luckily, ground ivy has a very low tolerance for boron, while turfgrass (and oddly some other weeds typically found in lawns—like dandelions and quackgrass) can survive greater amounts. Dr. Hatterman-Valenti warns against treating vegetable gardens or perennial beds with boron. "We just don't know how various vegetables and ornamental plants will be affected by this treatment—especially at a young age."

So if your ground ivy is in the vegetable garden, you'll just have to keep hoeing and pulling. Be especially aggressive in the springtime before it starts actively growing, and try to pull up all the roots you can. If you want to try the borax solution on your lawn, we'll tell you how. Just promise that you won't use it more than once a year or for more than a couple years total. (*Note:* Readers who live where boron is already present in the soil at high levels, such as the West Coast, shouldn't use it at all; you could kill all your plants.)

You agree to the rules? All right, here 'tis. The best time to spray is in the fall. Mix 2 teaspoons of borax with 1 quart of hot water, and stir well. Apply this solution with a sprayer to exactly 25 square feet of ground ivy-infested lawn, covering as much of the ground ivy leaves as possible. Resist the temptation to use more borax; it could damage your lawn.

This treatment should get rid of about 90 percent of the ground ivy. Pull or hoe out any survivors.

Doddering On

Q: My lawns and pasture of mixed grass and clover have been attacked by dodder, a parasitic weed. The weed has a strong foothold in 2 of my 5 acres, and my extension agent has told me the only way to control and eliminate it is to spray all 5 acres with herbicide. Are there any ways to fight this weed organically?

A: We asked Steve Orloff, a University of California farm advisor and one of the country's leading dodder experts, about how to control this pernicious weed in your pasture. He says that as soon as you finish reading this, beg, borrow, or steal a flame weeder. Take it out to your pasture and torch any remnants of dodder you see. You want to destroy any dodder seeds before they fall to the ground, where they can remain viable for years.

Next year, any seeds that are already lurking in your ground will sprout, sending up little tendrils that will attach themselves to host plants in your pasture and suck the life out of them. Orloff recommends cutting your pasture with a flail mower sometime before July, when the dodder will form seeds again. Flail mowers cut very close to the ground and, you hope, below the dodder, which can regrow from the tiniest smidgen of a piece.

Let the pasture cuttings lie, and the sun will bake the life out of the parasite. Next fall, do the flame weeder thing again. "If you keep at it, you can get dodder under control this way,"

CHECK IT **OUT!**

Kudzu and purple loose-strife are just two examples of plants that were intro-duced to North America from other continents with good intentions—but then began to invade natural areas. Many other invasive plants also threaten our wildlands. One way that you can help to slow the invasion is to learn which plants are a problem in your area and eliminate them from your plantings. To learn more about invasive plants, contact your nearest natural park or visit the Natural Park Service Web site: www.aqd.nps.gov

says Orloff. That is, as long as you don't let your horses eat it. "Animals spread the weed very well," warns Orloff. "The seeds pass through their digestive tract just fine."

Curse of the Kudzu

Q: *How do you get rid of kudzu? Its roots are either too hard and thick to dig up, or they are entangled with the roots of my plants. How can I get it out of my garden without hurting my plants?*

A: You *can* kill this monster weed (recognized by its angular, ivy-shaped, dark green leaves and grapevinelike growth)—by hacking away at it with persistence. "Cut it off at the base, *keep* cutting off all of its new growth, and it will eventually die," assures William S. Curran, Ph.D., extension agronomist at Penn State University. Be sure to also pull up any new little kudzu plants that sprout from seed, and within 3 or 4 years your garden should be kudzu-free, predicts Dr. Curran.

Kudzu is especially troublesome in the South, where it was planted *on purpose* to control erosion—and then be-came *flora nongrata* by smothering roads, railroads, forests, and anything else in its path. "I have heard of people making lamp stands out of kudzu roots down here in the South, but I don't know if the roots get *that* big up in the North," relates Ford Eastin, Ph.D., professor of weed science at the University of Georgia—who adds that *goats* will be happy to eat that kudzu (and, unfortunately, the rest of your garden as well) right down to the ground for you.

Losing Loosestrife

Q: *I read an article in* Organic Gardening *magazine about the horticultural war on purple loosestrife by the U.S. Fish and Wildlife Service. I have been* *waging my own war for 2 years, ever since I bought a gooseneck loosestrife as a 50-cent "bargain" at a garden market sale. The article says that the service requests homeowners to "eradicate" any known or suspected ornamental plantings of purple loosestrife. What do they mean by eradicate? What can be done to control the plant besides digging because I am weary of digging?*

A: We don't suppose it will ease your aching back to hear that purple loosestrife can be much more invasive than your gooseneck loosestrife. Actually, they are different plants completely. Gooseneck loosestrife (*Lysimachia clethroides*) has white flowers that look like little goose heads; the flowers of purple loosestrife (*Lythrum salicaria*) are straight, hot-pink spikes.

Gooseneck loosestrife is a good groundcover for wet areas, but it will quickly take over a mixed perennial border, says Alan Summers, president of Carroll Gardens in Westminster, Maryland. It spreads by underground stolons, so digging or smothering them with an impenetrable mulch or cover are the best remedies. Give the roots away to someone who needs to combat an erosion problem or burn them if you can. You may be able to keep your own personal loosestrife from spreading farther by sinking some kind of shallow barrier around the perimeter of its area, according to Summers.

For those of you dealing with purple loosestrife, we offer these tips from Richard Malecki, Ph.D., research biologist with the U.S. Fish and Wildlife Service, stationed at Cornell University:

"Dig up the whole plant. If you leave part of the root, it will sprout. A piece of the stem will sprout if that piece sits in water," he adds. After you've dug it up, dry the plant in the sun on a hard surface like a driveway until you're sure the pieces are completely lifeless. You can compost the pieces if your pile is hot and active.

Do everything you can to keep the seeds from spreading—one plant can produce thousands of seeds. Cut the seed-heads before they ripen. Learn to identify young plants so you can pull them when they are small and easier to handle.

Dr. Malecki does offer some hope for the future, by the way. Thanks to his work seeking biological controls for loosestrife, two beetles and a weevil that feed on the plant have been introduced from Europe. The insects have already been released in seven states and Canada and, if all goes well, they may one day help free our wetlands and streams of this purple menace.

Wild Rose Woes

Q: *The site where I wish to plant my new garden is covered with well-established weeds, including wild roses. An agricultural extension agent told me to use an herbicide in spring, then till. The garden will be near our well. Is there another way to do this job? Would a mulch of chipped wood and shredded leaves kill the weeds? Any solution that you suggest must be something a skinny 43-year-old woman can do by herself. (My husband will only garden in sub-freezing temperatures because then it becomes a survival sport.)*

A: Of course, you don't need toxic herbicides to get rid of those nasty wild roses. But you will need to be patient. Water the area you're going to clear thoroughly, then grab hold of the stems (wearing thick gloves, of course), and pull gently; the underground root system should pull out for you.

It's like pulling up a buried telephone wire—keep pulling until you get stuck; you're probably at a root ball. Get a shovel or trowel, uncover as much of this central root as you can, and then dig it up (if you can't get it all, try to mangle it up a lot). Don't try to do it all in one day, and don't get discouraged. When you're done (or just can't do anymore), it's time for step two.

Spread a thick layer of chipped wood and shredded leaves at least 6 inches deep over the area you want to clear. Wet it down, then cover it with something really impenetrable, like black plastic, old carpet, a swimming pool liner, or a couple inches of black and white newspaper. Anchor the cover well. Wait a year.

"The mulch will compost, the wild roses will die, *and* the soil will be improved," explains Frank Gouin, Ph.D., chair of the horticulture department at the University of Maryland. Next spring, remove the cover, till in the composted mulch, and plant your garden.

Those wild roses (most likely the dreaded multiflora rose), once touted as something you should plant to create a living fence until it revealed its tendency to spread rampantly, are tough. Keep pulling up any new sprouts that appear after your cover comes off (get those missed roots, too), and the plants will eventually die. These "rosebushes" have *big* root systems and may sprout up anywhere; get 'em when they do.

LAWNS & LANDSCAPES

Lawn and landscape problems can be among the most perplexing for gardeners. After all, what do you do about those brown spots courtesy of Fido, or the fact that you can't get anything to grow under your black walnut trees? Don't despair—in this chapter, you'll discover the answers to these questions—and more.

LAWN CARE
Bad Dogs & Old Salts

Q: *How can I restore brown spots on the lawn caused by dog urine and snow-melting salts? Also, is there a balanced liquid organic fertilizer? I am trying to find a substitute for Miracle-Gro for my 20 × 20-foot vegetable garden and flowerbeds, and unfortunately, I don't have the facilities to make manure tea.*

A: Lawns turn brown where dogs leave a liquid message because there's lots of nitrogen in urine. Too much nitrogen can burn a lawn (or any plant) whether in the form of urine or too much chemical fertilizer, says Tom Palmieri of Nature's Green in Blairstown, New Jersey, a lawn-care company with an organic program.

To dilute that nitrogen concentration, keep an eye on your dog and have a hose handy to soak the spot heavily immediately after the act. Unfortunately, says Palmieri, "dogs have a tendency to go to the same spot over and over because they are marking their territory. If you can keep them moving around instead, the grass may be able to outgrow its nitrogen overload. Most grass can survive one wet spot a week," he says.

To *restore* a burned-out spot, rake up the dead grass and 1 inch or so of soil, then replace it with top soil and a little compost. Sow grass seed, cover it with a thin layer of straw, and keep it moist (and keep your dog off it) until the seed sprouts and becomes well established—same goes for salt-damaged areas. In spring, rake away as much soil, debris, and dead grass as possible, and dispose of it; replant as above, and water a lot to wash away remaining salt.

If *you* are the cause of salt problem, consider using calcium chloride, a less salty product. It's a little more expensive, but it won't kill your grass as quickly. If your front lawn is at the mercy of your municipality, consider replanting it with a tall fescue such as a *Puccinellia* species, says Palmieri.

You can also add a little gypsum to your soil if it's alkaline or lime if it's acidic. Harry L. Motto, Ph.D., a soil scientist at Rutgers University, says that these substances speed up the rate at which the sodium leaches from the soil. Have your soil tested for pH and soluble salts, then ask your local cooperative extension for advice on how much to mix into the soil before you replant.

As for the liquid fertilizer, we first feel obligated to remind you that a spray of *any* kind is no substitute for fertile soil. If you don't have the space to compost personally, you are almost certainly close to some municipal source of free compost. A nice big batch mixed into your soil a couple weeks before planting each year should help your garden get off its liquid fix. If your garden needs a little more nitrogen (remember to get that soil test first), you can use a liquid spray of fish emulsion and water, or a seaweed or kelp spray that will also provide vital micronutrients you won't find in any green-colored chemical!

Out, Brown Patch

Q: *We have a turfgrass problem. Every year patches of our lawn turn brown when the first heat wave hits in June. Every fall we dig these areas up and plant tall fescue ('Arid' or 'Rebel' varieties), and the new grass does well until the next June, when the same thing happens again. We identified our problem* as **"brown patch," caused by Rhizoctonia solani. We tried a sulfur fungicide but that didn't help for long. Any suggestions?**

A: Be assured that your lawn isn't the only patchy one around. Houston Couch, Ph.D., turfgrass pathologist at Virginia Polytechnic Institute, says first, don't overwater; keep your lawn as dry as possible. "Rhizoctonia is a wet weather disease," he explains. "If the grass stays wet for 48 hours straight, the disease will really take off, so do everything you can to keep it dry." When your lawn *does* need water, water at night when the grass is wet anyway (and when *everyone* should water their lawn, regardless of locale).

Second, fertilize your lawn in the fall, but go easy on the amount of nitrogen you add. "The disease is made more severe by high nitrogen levels," says Dr. Couch. And third, raise the cutting height on your lawn mower. When you mow your grass, cut it no shorter than 2½ to 3 inches, which is the right height for tall fescue.

Dr. Couch says that the 'Rebel' seed you're using *is* one of the most rhizoctonia-resistant grass varieties you can grow. A variety with even more resistance is 'Houndog' (no kidding, that's its name—and how you spell it); you can order it from a lawn and garden center near you. And you probably don't need to dig and replant your lawn every fall, adds Dr. Couch. Try some "dog" this fall and then leave it alone for awhile. "It should come back by itself just fine," he says.

St. Augustine Invasion

Q: *We installed a sod lawn about 7 years ago. It's a mix of 'Olympia' bluegrass and tall fescue. Now it's being overtaken by St. Augustinegrass, a pesky weed that sends out runners over the top of the sod. I've*

tried to pull it out but it spreads more and more. Would either cutting the lawn real short or leaving it tall help?

A: Cut the grass short, says James R. Brooks, executive director of the Lawn Institute (www.lawninstitute.com) in Marietta, Georgia, who suggests mowing your besieged lawn to 1¼ inches high. "St. Augustinegrass likes to grow higher," he says, adding that the best time to go short is in the spring or fall.

LANDSCAPE QUESTIONS

Hardy Climbers

Q: *What climbing vines will grow in poor, rocky soil? I need one that will conceal, and possibly cool, a 40-foot tower.*

A: "Trumpet vine (*Campsis radicans*) is your best bet," says Michael Dirr, Ph.D., professor of ornamental horticulture at the University of Georgia in Athens, and author of *Manual of Woody Landscape Plants* (Stipes Publishing, 1998). "*Campsis* tolerates cold temperatures and grows like a weed. I'd suggest either the yellow-flowered 'Flava' or the red-flowered 'Crimson Trumpet'. Both are widely available." Trumpet vine grows 30 to 40 feet in nearly any soil, has lush foliage, and flowers from summer into fall.

"Another possibility is akebia," he says. "It's more cold-hardy than people give it credit for." Any lush vine will help cool the tower by shading it, adds Dr. Dirr.

Planting a Butterfly Garden

Q: *What are the best plants to include in a garden to attract butterflies?*

A: Butterflies subsist mostly on flower nectars and will come to an environment with a variety of plants and flowers and some moisture. They prefer vibrant colors such as red, orange, yellow, and blue, although they're drawn to other colors, notes Ruth Shaw Ernst in her book *The Naturalist's Garden* (Rodale, 1987).

To establish a real butterfly garden, dedicate a sunny part of the backyard to wildflowers and the garden flowers (listed below) that butterflies are most drawn to. Let the patch get overgrown, and allow it to self-sow. Keep a spot or two moist or puddly, or set out a dish of water to provide that important moisture source. Include a few flat stones or a slate for these beautiful creatures to sun themselves on.

Bee balm, cosmos, morning glory, phlox, sedum, and verbena are some of butterflies' favorite garden flowers. They also prefer aster, butterfly bush (*Buddleia*), butterfly weed (of course!), cornflower, bush honeysuckle, lilac, mimosa, and thistle. A butterfly's long, coiled tongue is able to probe deep into flowers for food.

In addition to nectar, they will also feast on rotting, fermenting fruit and oozing tree sap. Monarch and queen butterflies prefer to lay eggs on milkweed, while swallowtails choose carrot, dill, and parsley. When the eggs hatch, the foliage of choice is right there for emerging larvae to eat.

Remember that the downside of butterflies is their plant-eating progeny. Luckily, their predatory and parasitic enemies, which are attracted by many of the same plantings, generally keep them under control. Any larvae that survive attacks by insects, wasps, flies, birds, frogs, toads, and spiders will grow and shed their skins four to six times as they become bigger. Then they enter the chrysalis or pupal stage, a stage in which they are generally immobile. Finally, a beautiful adult emerges to breed a new generation.

Too Much Moss?

Q: *How can I eliminate the moss growing on the walkways between my raised beds? The paths are 18 inches wide, and the beds are made with cedar boards.*

A: Many gardeners like the emerald color and velvety texture of moss; shade gardeners often encourage its growth. Instead of eliminating the moss, take advantage of its ornamental qualities, suggests Parker Andes, landscape superintendent at Longwood Gardens in Kennett Square, Pennsylvania. Construct a stone path over the existing walk, and allow the moss to fill the crevices between the stones.

If you'd really rather not have the moss, widen the paths to admit more light and allow faster evaporation, since moss grows in moist, shady, acidic soil. Loosen the soil with a cultivator, spread a layer of lime to raise the pH, then mulch with a 3- to 6-inch layer of wood chips or bark. You also could mulch with grass clippings or straw, but these decompose more quickly and are less attractive.

TREE TRICKS

Black Walnut Woes

Q: *After 8 years of using compost and cover crops, avoiding synthetic pesticides and fertilizers, and learning not to scream when I found a garter snake in* the garden, nothing was thriving. The soil is a beautiful, rich, loamy, chocolate cake-type, but it doesn't produce. A recent article about nuts in your magazine finally explained why. There is an abundance of walnut trees near my garden. Unfortunately, they're on a neighbor's property. Choices for relocating my garden are very limited. Any suggestions?

Q: *I need a list of edibles and ornamentals that tolerate juglone, the naturally occurring chemical in black walnut trees that stunts the growth of other plants. These trees are ubiquitous where I live in the Blue Ridge Mountains, and it is impossible to avoid them.*

What about English walnut trees and leaves? Are they allelopathic (suppress growth) as well?

A: Jerry Van Sambeek, Ph.D., research plant physiologist at the U.S. Forest Service in Carbondale, Illinois, says that yes, juglone is also produced by the English walnut and by other closely related trees—pecans, hickories, and butternuts—but to a lesser extent.

Tomatoes, potatoes, alfalfa, apples, blackberries, rhododendrons, azaleas, mountain laurels, and pines seem to be the most sensitive to juglone, according to various researchers who have looked at this problem over the years. Sweet peppers, lilacs, viburnums, autumn crocus, peonies, magnolias, and crabapples are also sensitive, but not as much.

The good news is that some plants can grow normally (some even better) near a black walnut tree. Snap beans, lima beans, onions, parsnips, sweet corn, dandelion, black raspberries, grapes, and mints don't mind the trees; neither do a wide variety of grasses (including Kentucky bluegrass and timothy), white clover and other legumes, wild roses, forsythia, Virginia creeper, narcissus, goldenrod, marigolds, violets, ferns, red cedar, and virtually all native hardwoods.

How far from a tree does the effect of its juglone extend? That depends on how big the tree is and how far its roots extend from its center (usually about one and a half times the height of the tree). Researchers have shown that it's contact with walnut roots that most adversely affects other plants, so plants with very shallow root systems that do not touch walnut roots may be able to grow near the tree without ill effects. (The deep-rooted plants we mentioned earlier are somehow able to withstand the strong effects of juglone despite their roots' contact with it.)

Juglone is found throughout the tree, and leaves can carry the naturally occurring chemical into the soil. But juglone breaks down quickly in well-aerated soil with lots of microbial activity. Severe juglone problems are most likely to occur on poorly drained soils. If the soil beneath a walnut tree is deep, fertile, and full of organic matter, you might even be able to grow tomatoes there, says Dr. Van Sambeek.

By the way, the amount of juglone produced can vary from tree to tree. If nothing grows beneath the branches of a specific black walnut, you may have a real killer tree on your hands. Juglone production also increases when the tree is under stress, such as that produced by a lack of moisture. Keeping walnut trees well watered may help you to grow other plants beneath them more easily.

Should you add leaves from black walnut trees to your compost heap? Yes, if the mix isn't too heavy on black walnut leaves, the bacteria in your pile will break down the juglone.

Unruly Roots

Q: *When we purchased our home, the lawn was already planted with a large number of some type of hybrid poplar that put out huge, unsightly roots above ground. They extend 10 to 15 feet from the trunk in every direction and we're unable to run a lawn mower around any of the trees. We rely on the trees for shade and would hate to cut them down. Do you have any suggestions?*

A: Your best option might be to plant root-hiding shrubs or groundcovers under your trees. Mark Nash, Ph.D., assistant professor of ornamental horticulture at the University of Tennessee, suggests winter creeper euonymus (*Euonymus fortunei*). Although some trees are more prone to aboveground roots than others, excessive watering, compacted soil, or too much mulch can aggravate the problem, he says, because tree roots need oxygen to survive. Experts agree that burying them with soil or cutting the roots is unlikely to solve the problem either.

Understory Glory

Q: *I have two liquidambar and two California redwood trees in my backyard. What kind of plants can I grow under them? The plants would have to tolerate tree roots, dry soil, and part shade.*

A: "Azaleas and rhododendrons might do nicely under a redwood because they are acid-loving plants and the redwood foliage that would fall to the ground beneath the tree would be acidic," says Ursula Schuch, Ph.D., horticulturist at the University of California in Riverside. "Check with a local nursery for varieties of azaleas and rhododendrons that will do well in your area," she advises.

Plant the shrubs at least 3 to 4 feet away from the trunk of the redwoods, and be careful when you do, she cautions: "Redwoods don't take too well to having their root systems disturbed. Don't dig any more than you have to."

Liquidambar trees, on the other hand, have large root systems that "I wouldn't be too concerned about disturbing," says Dr. Schuch, adding that "it's still a good idea to stay at least 3 to 4 feet from the trunk." Consider planting small spring-blooming bulbs or grass beneath the liquidambar trees. Heuchera (coral bells) should do well under either the redwoods *or* the liquidambar trees, she adds.

Some more suggestions for under both trees from John Karlik, a farm advisor with the Kern County Cooperative Extension in Bakersfield, California: groundcovers such as wild strawberries and star jasmine *(Trachelospermum jasminoides).* "Star jasmine is very common here," he explains. "It's a good, fragrant groundcover that will grow about 1½ feet tall." You could also plant shade-loving annuals such as begonias, he adds.

Putting Trees to Bed

Q: *I'd like to put some raised beds around my trees, but don't want to kill the trees by smothering their roots. How deep can the soil be?*

A: Surrounding the base of a tree with a 2- to 3-inch layer of soil that drains well should not harm the tree. But avoid building the bed with heavy clay soil, black plastic, or similar materials that could suffocate roots growing close to the surface, says Thomas Green, Ph.D., urban forestry professor at Western Illinois University. If you top the bed with mulch, choose one that allows water and oxygen to pass through easily.

RESOURCES

Vegetables: Seeds & Plants

Bountiful Gardens
18001 Shafer Ranch Road
Willits, CA 95490
Phone/fax: (707) 459-6410
E-mail: bountiful@zapcom.net
Web site: www.bountiful
gardens.org

W. Atlee Burpee
300 Park Avenue
Warminster, PA 18974
Phone: (800) 888-1447;
(800) 333-5808
Fax (800) 487-5530
E-mail: burpeecs@surfnet
work.net
Web site: www.burpee.com

Companion Plants
7247 North Coolville
Ridge Road
Athens, OH 45701
Phone: (740) 592-4643
Fax: (740) 593-3092
E-mail: complants@frognet.net
Web site: www.frognet.net/
companionplants/

The Cook's Garden
P.O. Box 535
Londonderry, VT 05148
Phone: (800) 457-9703
Fax: (800) 457-9705
E-mail: gardener@cooks
garden.com
Web site:
www.cooksgarden.com

William Dam Seeds Ltd.
P.O. Box 8400
Dundas, ON L9H 6M1
Canada
Phone: (905) 628-6641
Fax: (905) 627-1729
E-mail: willdam@sympatico.ca
Web site: www.damseeds.com

Fedco Seeds
P.O. Box 520
Waterville, ME 04903
Phone: (207) 873-7333
Fax: (207) 872-8317
E-mail: fedco@mint.net

Ferry-Morse Seeds
P.O. Box 1620
Fulton, KY 42041
Phone: (800) 283-3400
Fax: (270) 472-3402
E-mail: webmaster
@ferry-morse.com
Web site: www.ferry-morse.com

Henry Field's Seed &
Nursery Co.
415 North Burnett
Shenandoah, IA 51602
Phone: (605) 665-9391
Fax: (605) 665-2601
E-mail: info@henryfields.com
Web site: www.henryfields.com

Filaree Farm
182 Conconully Highway
Okanogan, WA 98840
Phone: (509) 422-6940
E-mail: filaree@north
cascades.net
Web site: www.filareefarm.com

Garden City Seeds
778 Highway 93 North
Hamilton, MT 59840
Phone: (406) 961-4837
Fax: (406) 961-4877
E-mail: seeds@montana.com
Web site: www.gardencity
seeds.com

Heritage Seed Company
HC 78, Box 187
Star City, AR 71667
Phone: (870) 628-4820
E-mail: questions@daylilies.net

J. L. Hudson, Seedsman
SR 2, Box 337
LaHonda, CA 94020

Ed Hume Seeds
P.O. Box 1450
Kent, WA 98035
Fax: (253) 859-0694
E-mail: humeseeds@aol.com
Web site:
www.humeseeds.com

Irish Eyes with a Hint of Garlic
P.O. Box 307
Ellensburg, WA 98926
Phone: (509) 925-6025
Fax: (800) 964-9210
E-mail: potatoes
@irish-eyes.com
Web site: www.irish-eyes.com

Johnny's Selected Seeds
Foss Hill Road
Albion, ME 04910
Phone: (207) 437-4357
Fax: (207) 437-2165;
   (800) 437-4290
E-mail: johnnys@johnny
   seeds.com
Web site:
   www.johnnyseeds.com

J. W. Jung Seed Co.
335 South High Street
Randolph, WI 53957
Phone: (800) 297-3123
Fax: (800) 692-5864
E-mail: info@jungseed.com
Web site: www.jungseed.com

Native Seeds/SEARCH
526 North 4th Avenue
Tucson, AZ 85705-8450
Phone: (520) 622-5561
Fax: (520) 622-5591
E-mail: nss@azstarnet.com
Web site:
   ww.azstarnet.com/~nss

Nichols Garden Nursery
1190 North Pacific Highway
   NE
Albany, OR 97321
Phone: (541) 928-9280
Fax: (541) 967-8406
E-mail:
   info@gardennursery.com
Web site: www.garden
   nursery.com

Park Seed Company
1 Parkton Avenue
Greenwood, SC 29647
Phone: (864) 223-8555;
   (800) 845-3369
Fax: (864) 941-4206;
   (800) 275-9941
E-mail: orders@parkseed.com
Web site: www.parkseed.com

Pinetree Garden Seeds
P.O. Box 300
616A Lewiston Road
New Gloucester, ME 04260
Phone: (207) 926-3400
Fax: (888) 527-3337
E-mail:
   superseeds@worldnet.att.net
Web site:
   www.superseeds.com

Sand Hill Preservation Center
1878 230th Street
Calamus, IA 52729

Seed Savers Heirloom Seeds
   and Gifts
(Seed Saver's Exchange)
3076 North Winn Road
Decorah, IA 52101
Phone: (319) 382-5990
Fax: (319) 382-5872

Seeds Trust, High Altitude
   Gardens
P.O. Box 1048
Hailey, ID 83333-1048
Phone: (208) 788-4363
Fax: (208) 788-3452
E-mail: higarden@micron.net
Web site: www.seedsave.org

Shepherd's Garden Seeds
30 Irene Street
Torrington, CT 06790
Phone: (860) 482-3638
Fax: (860) 482-0532
E-mail: custsrv@shepherd
   seeds.com
Web site: www.shepherd
   seeds.com

R. H. Shumway, Seedsman
P.O. Box 1
Graniteville, SC 29829
Phone: (803) 663-9771
Fax: (888) 437-2733
Web site:
   www.rhshumway.com

Southern Exposure Seed
   Exchange
P.O. Box 170
Earlysville, VA 22936
Phone: (804) 973-4703
Fax: (804) 973-8717
E-mail: gardens@southern
   exposure.com
Web site: www.southern
   exposure.com

Territorial Seed Co.
P.O. Box 157
Cottage Grove, OR 97424
Phone: (541) 942-9547
Fax: (888) 657-3131
E-mail: tertr1@srvl.vsite.com
Web site:
   www.territorial-seed.com

Tomato Growers Supply
   Company
P.O. Box 2237
Fort Myers, FL 33902
Phone: (941) 768-1119;
   (888) 478-7333
Fax: (888) 768-3476
Web site:
   www.tomatogrowers.com

Vermont Bean Seed Co.
Garden Lane
Fair Haven, VT 05743
Phone: (803) 663-0217
Fax: (888) 500-7333
Web site:
   www.vermontbean.com

Well-Sweep Herb Farm
205 Mount Bethel Road
Port Murray, NJ 07865
Phone: (908) 852-5390
Fax: (908) 852-1649

Willhite Seed, Inc.
P.O. Box 23
Poolville, TX 76487
Phone: (817) 599-8656
Fax: (817) 599-5843
E-mail: info@willhiteseed.com
Web site: willhiteseed.com

Fruit: Plants & Interest Groups

Bear Creek Nursery
P.O. Box 411
Northport, WA 99157
Phone: (509) 732-6219
Fax: (509) 732-4417
E-mail: BearCreek@plix.com
Web site:
   www.BearCreekNursery.com

Four Winds Growers
P.O. Box 3538
Fremont, CA 94539
Phone: (510) 656-2591
Fax: (510) 656-1360
E-mail: fourwinds@mother.com
Web site:
   www.fourwindsgrowers.com

North American Fruit Explorers
1716 Apples Road
Chapin, IL 62628
Phone: (217) 245-7589
Fax: (217) 245-7844
E-mail: vorbeck@csj.net
Web site: www.nafex.org

Park Seed Company
1 Parkton Avenue
Greenwood, SC 29647
Phone: (864) 223-8555;
   (800) 845-3369
Fax: (864) 941-4206;
   (800) 275-9941
E-mail: orders@parkseed.com
Web site: www.parkseed.com

St. Lawrence Nurseries
325 State Highway 345
Potsdam, NY 13676
Phone: (315) 265-6739
E-mail: trees@sln.potsdam.ny.us
Web site:
   www.sln.potsdam.ny.us

Stark Brothers Nursery
P.O. Box 10
Louisiana, MO 63353
Phone: (800) 478-2759
Fax: (573) 754-5290
E-mail: service@starkbros.com
Web site: www.starkbros.com

Van Well Nursery
P.O. Box 1339
Wenatchee, WA 98807
Phone: (509) 886-8189;
   (800) 572-1553
Fax: (509) 886-0294
E-mail: vanwell@vanwell.net
Web site: www.vanwell.net

Ornamentals: Bulbs, Plants & Seeds

Bluestone Perennials
7211 Middle Ridge Road
Madison, OH 44057
Phone: (440) 428-7535;
   (800) 852-5243
Fax: (440) 428-7198
E-mail: bluestone@bluestone
   perennials.com
Web site: www.bluestone
   perennials.com

Brent and Becky's Bulbs
7463 Heath Trail
Gloucester, VA 23061
Phone: (877) 661-2852;
   (804) 693-3966
Fax: (804) 693-9436
E-mail: store@brentandbeckys
   bulbs.com
Web site: www.brentandbeckys
   bulbs.com

Bundles of Bulbs
PNB 349
1498 M Reisterstown Road
Baltimore, MD 21208
Phone: (410) 581-2188
Fax: (215) 862-3696

Busse Gardens
17160 245th Avenue
Big Lake, MN 55309
Phone: (612) 263-3403
Fax: (612) 263-1473
E-mail: customer.service
    @bussegardens.com
Web site:
    www.bussegardens.com

Flowery Branch Seed Company
P.O. Box 1330
Flowery Branch, GA 30542
Phone: (770) 536-8380
Fax: (770) 532-7825
E-mail: seedsman@mind-
    spring.com
Web site: www.flowerybranch
    seeds.com

Goodwin Creek Gardens
P.O. Box 83
Williams, OR 97544
Phone/fax: (541) 846-7357
E-mail: goodwincreek
    @terragon.com
Web site: www.goodwincreek
    gardens.com

Heard Gardens Ltd.
5355 Merle Hay Road
Johnston, IA 50131
Phone: (515) 276-4533
Fax: (515) 276-8322
E-mail:
    info@heardgardens.com
Web site:
    www.heardgardens.com

Heritage Seed Company
HC 78, Box 187
Star City, AR 71667
Phone: (870) 628-4820
E-mail: questions@daylilies.net

J. L. Hudson, Seedsman
SR 2, Box 337
LaHonda, CA 94020

Logee's Greenhouses
141 North Street
Danielson, CT 06239
Phone: (888) 330-8038;
    (860) 774-8038
Fax: (888) 774-9932
E-mail: logee-info@logees.com
Web site: www.logees.com

Midwest Wildflowers
P.O. Box 64
Rockton, IL 61072
Phone: (815) 624-7040

Milaeger's Gardens
4838 Douglas Avenue
Racine, WI 53402-2498
Phone: (262) 639-2040;
    (800) 669-1229
Fax: (262) 639-1855
E-mail: milaeger@execpc.com
Web site: www.milaegers.com

Niche Gardens
1111 Dawson Road
Chapel Hill, NC 27516
Phone: (919) 967-0078
Fax: (919) 967-4026
E-mail: orders@nichegdn.com
Web site: www.nichegdn.com

Richters
357 Highway 47
Goodwood, ON
LOC 1AO Canada
Phone: (905) 640-6677
Fax: (905) 640-6641
E-mail: inquiry@richters.com
Web site: www.richters.com

Select Seeds Antique Flowers
180 Stickney Hill Road
Union, CT 06076
Phone: (860) 684-9310
Fax: (800) 653-3304
E-mail: info@selectseeds.com
Web site:
    www.selectseeds.com

Spangle Creek Labs
21950 County Road 445
Bovey, MN 55709
Phone: (218) 247-0245
Web site: www.uslink.net/~scl

Wayside Gardens
1 Garden Lane
Hodges, SC 29695-0001
Phone: (800) 845-1124
Fax: (800) 817-1124
E-mail: curator@wayside
    gardens.com
Web site: www.wayside
    gardens.wte.net

Well-Sweep Herb Farm
205 Mount Bethel Road
Port Murray, NJ 07865
Phone: (908) 852-5390
Fax: (908) 852-1649

White Flower Farm
P.O. Box 50
Litchfield, CT 06759
Phone: (800) 503-9624
Fax: (860) 496-1418
E-mail: custserv@whiteflower
    farm.com
Web site: www.whiteflower
    farm.com

Organic Gardening Supplies

A. M. Leonard, Inc.
241 Fox Drive
Piqua, OH 45356-0816
Phone: (800) 543-8955
Fax: (800) 443-0633
E-mail: info@amleo.com
Web site: www.amleo.com

The Beneficial Insect Co.
137 Forrest Street
Fort Mill, SC 29715
Phone: (803) 547-2301
E-mail: info@bugfarm.com
Web site: www.bugfarm.com

AgAccess/ Fertile Ground Books
P.O. Box 2008
Davis, CA 95617-2008
Phone: (530) 297-7879;
    (800) 540-0170
Fax: (530) 298-2060
E-mail: books@agribooks.com
Web site: www.agribooks.com

Gardener's Supply Company
128 Intervale Road
Burlington, VT 05401
Phone: (800) 863-1700
Fax: (800) 551-6712
E-mail: info@gardeners.com
Web site: www.gardeners.com

Gardens Alive!
5100 Schenley Place
Lawrenceburg, IN 47025
Phone: (812) 537-8650
Fax: (812) 537-5108
E-mail: gardenhelp@gardens-
    alive.com
Web site:
    www.gardens-alive.com

Harmony Farm Supply & Nursery
P.O. Box 460
Graton, CA 95444
Phone: (707) 823-9125
Fax: (707) 823-1734
E-mail: info@harmonyfarm.com
Web site:
    www.harmonyfarm.com

Kinsman Garden Company, Inc.
River Road
P.O. Box 357
Point Pleasant, PA 18950-0357
Phone: (215) 297-0890;
    (800) 733-4146
Fax: (215) 297-0450
E-mail:
    kinsmangarden@bux.com
Web site: www.kinsman
    garden.com

Lehman's Catalog
P.O. Box 41
Kidron, OH 44636
Phone: (330) 857-5757
Fax: (330) 857-5785
E-mail: info@lehmans.com
Web site: www.lehmans.com

Natural Insect Control
RR #2
Stevensville, ON L0S 1S0
Canada
Phone: (905) 382-2904
Fax: (905) 382-4418
E-mail: nic@niagara.com
Web site: www.natural-insect-
    control.com

Peaceful Valley Farm Supply
P.O. Box 2209
Grass Valley, CA 95945
Phone: (888) 784-1722;
    (530) 272-4769
Fax: (530) 272-4794
E-mail:
    contact@groworganic.com
Web site:
    www.groworganic.com

Planet Natural
1612 Gold Avenue
Bozeman, MT 59715
Phone: (800) 289-6656;
    (406) 587-5891
Fax: (406) 587-0223
E-mail: ecostore@mcn.net
Web site:
    www.planetnatural.com

H. B. Sherman Traps, Inc.
3731 Peddie Drive
Tallahassee, FL 32303
Phone: (850) 575-8727
Fax: (850) 575-4864
E-mail:
    traps@shermantraps.com
Web site:
    www.shermantraps.com

RECOMMENDED READING

Ball, Jeff, and Liz Ball. *Rodale's Flower Garden Problem Solver*. Emmaus, PA: Rodale, 1994.

Bradley, Fern Marshall, ed. *Gardening with Perennials*. Emmaus, PA: Rodale, 1996.

Bradley, Fern Marshall, and Barbara W. Ellis, eds. *Rodale's All-New Encyclopedia of Organic Gardening*. Emmaus, PA: Rodale, 1992.

Cunningham, Sally Jean. *Great Garden Companions*. Emmaus, PA: Rodale, 1998.

Cutler, Karan Davis. *Burpee—The Complete Vegetable & Herb Gardener: A Guide to Growing Your Garden Organically*. New York: Macmillan, 1997.

Coleman, Eliot. *The New Organic Grower: A Master's Manual of Tools and Techniques for the Home and Market Gardener*. 2nd ed. White River Junction, VT: Chelsea Green, 1995.

Gershuny, Grace. *Start with the Soil*. Emmaus, PA: Rodale, 1993.

Gilkeson, Linda, Pam Pierce, and Miranda Smith. *Rodale's Pest & Disease Problem Solver*. Emmaus, PA: Rodale, 1996.

Hupping, Carol, et al. *Stocking Up III*. New York: Fine Communications, 1995.

Lanza, Patricia. *Lasagna Gardening*. Emmaus, PA: Rodale, 1998.

Martin, Deborah L. *1,001 Ingenious Gardening Ideas*. Emmaus, PA: Rodale, 1999.

Martin, Deborah L., and Grace Gershuny. *The Rodale Book of Composting*. Emmaus, PA: Rodale, 1992.

Michalak, Patricia S., and Cass Peterson. *Rodale's Successful Organic Gardening: Vegetables*. Emmaus, PA: Rodale, 1993.

National Gardening Association staff. *Gardening: The Complete Guide to Growing America's Favorite Fruits & Vegetables*. Reading, MA: Addison-Wesley, 1986.

Nick, Jean M. A., and Fern Marshall Bradley. *Growing Fruits & Vegetables Organically*. Emmaus, PA: Rodale, 1994.

Ogden, Shepherd. *Step by Step Organic Vegetable Gardening: The Gardening Classic Revised and Updated*. New York: Harper-Collins, 1992.

Olkowski, William, Sheila Darr, and Helga Olkowski. *The Gardener's Guide to Common-Sense Pest Control*. Newtown, CT: Taunton, 1996.

Organic Gardening magazine, Rodale, 33 East Minor Street, Emmaus, PA 18098.

Phillips, Ellen, and C. Colston Burrell. *Rodale's Illustrated Encyclopedia of Perennials*. Emmaus, PA: Rodale, 1993.

Phillips, Michael. *The Apple Grower: A Guide for the Organic Orchardist*. White River Junction, VT: Chelsea Green, 1998.

Powell, Eileen. *From Seed to Bloom: How to Grow Over 500 Annuals, Perennials & Herbs*. Pownal, VT: Storey, 1995.

Stell, Elizabeth P. *Secrets to Great Soil*. Pownal, VT: Storey, 1998.

INDEX

A

Acid soil, increasing pH, 165
Actinidia arguta
  failure to produce fruit, 104–5
  layering, 106
  pruning, 105–6
  vitamins and, 105
Addresses and Web sites
  Alternative Farming Systems
    Information Center, 5
  Appropriate Technology Transfer for
    Rural Areas (ATTRA), 4
  Association of Specialty Cut Flower
    Growers, 4
  ATTRA (Appropriate Technology
    Transfer for Rural Areas), 4
  Backyard Fruit Growers, 101
  Chile Pepper, 44
  City Farmer, 146
  International Herb Association, 4
  Lawn Institute, 227
  National Park Service, 218
  NCAP (Northwest Coalition for
    Alternatives to Pesticides), 213
  North American Fruit Explorers, 105
  Northwest Coalition for Alternatives to
    Pesticides (NCAP), 213
  OCIA (Organic Crop Improvement
    Association International), 4
  Organic Crop Improvement
    Association International (OCIA),
    4
  Organic Gardening, 100
  Resources, 234–38
  Scatterseed Project, 40
  Sterling International, 179
  Vermont Northeast Organic Farming
    Association, 101
  Wallace Laboratories, 170
  Washington State University, Bulletins
    Office, 206
  Wellscroft Farm Fence Systems, 200
Akebia, 227
Alkaline soil, acidifying, 149–50
Allergies, and bean leaves, 10–11
Alternaria leaf blight, and carrots,
  20–21
Animal pests
  cats, 202–3
  deer, 10, 200, 207
  mice, 92
  moose, 200
  rabbits, 200, 204–5
  raccoons, 200
  rats, 144–46

squirrels, 200–201, 204–5
  ultrasonic devices and, 199–201
  voles, 92, 204–6
Annatto
  growing, 119
  harvesting seeds of, 119–20
Ants, and corn, 22–23
Aphids
  and brassicas, 14
  and corn, 22–23
  and crucifers, 176–77
  and fertilizer, 153
  and hoverflies, 82–83
  and soap sprays, 57
  and water sprays, 185
Apples
  bearing patterns of, 102
  bitter pit, 103
  and cedar apple rust, 100
  'Delicious', 101–2
  'Enterprise', 98
  'GoldRush', 99
  growing organically, 98–100
  late frosts and, 90–91
  pollination problems and, 101–2
  pruning, 90–92
  scab and, 98–99
  scald , 103
  storing, 102–3
Apple tree borers, 93
Apricots
  growing from seed, 129–30
  late frosts and, 90–91
  pruning of, 90–91
Armyworms, and cabbage, 17
Ashes
  coal, 151
  wood, 158–59
Asparagus, 7–10
  crown rot and, 9, 10
  cutting, 7–8
  extending harvest, 8
  mulching, 9
  root rot and, 9
  salt and, 8–9, 10
  soil pH and, 9
  weeds and, 8–9
  yield decline, 9
August lily, fragrance, 85

B

Bacillus thuringiensis (BT), and cabbage,
  17–18
Bacillus thuringiensis var. *israelensis*
  (BTI), and mosquitoes, 190

Bacillus thuringiensis var. *kurstaki* (BTK)
  and caterpillars, 17
  and corn earworm, 26
  and European corn borers, 183
Bacillus thuringiensis var. *san diego* (BT
  var. *san diego*), 180–81
Basal rot, and garlic, 31–32
Basil
  'Globe', 114
  'Miniature', 114
Bay laurel, growing indoors, 114–15
Bean leaf beetle, 178
Beans
  kelp and, 161
  saving seeds, 131–32
Beans, butter, 33–34
Beans, green, 10–12
  allergies and, 10–11
  and bean leaf beetle, 178
  crop rotation and, 12
  diseases, 12
  inoculants and, 11–12
  and Mexican bean beetles, 178–79
Beans, lima, 33–34
Beets, watering needs, 7
Begonias, angelwing, 75
Beneficial insects
  herbs attractive to, 116
  and horticultural oil, 198–99
  lacewings, 176–77, 199
  ladybugs, 176–77, 179, 191, 199
    overwintering indoors, 181–82
  parasitic wasps, 191
  spiders, 191
  spined soldier bugs, 179
Beneficial mites, and horticultural oil,
  198–99
Beneficial nematodes, 183–84
Bermuda grass, controlling, 213–14
Birds
  encouraging, 206
  protecting grapes from, 202
  protecting nut trees from, 201
Bitter pit, of apples, 103
Bixa orellana
  growing, 119
  harvesting seeds, 119–20
Black knot, of plums, 110–11
Black rot
  and carrots, 20–21
  and grapes, 103–4
  and sweet potatoes, 53–54
Bloodmeal, 158–59
Blossom-end rot, and tomatoes, 56
Bonemeal, 158–59
  as fertilizer, 152–53
  and mad cow disease, 153

USDA Plant Hardiness Zone Map

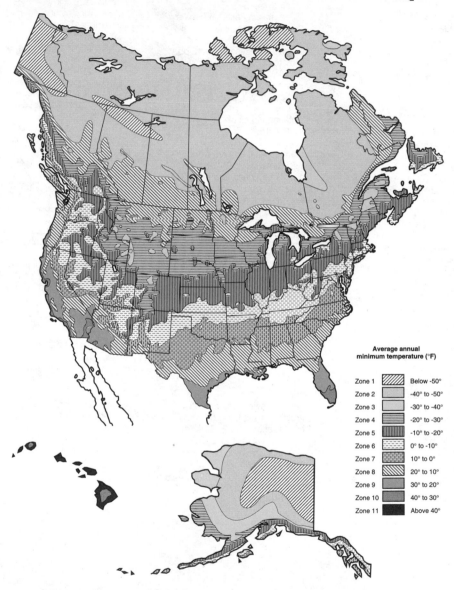

Average annual minimum temperature (°F)

Zone 1		Below -50°
Zone 2		-40° to -50°
Zone 3		-30° to -40°
Zone 4		-20° to -30°
Zone 5		-10° to -20°
Zone 6		0° to -10°
Zone 7		10° to 0°
Zone 8		20° to 10°
Zone 9		30° to 20°
Zone 10		40° to 30°
Zone 11		Above 40°

This map was revised in 1990 and is recognized as the best indicator of minimum temperatures available. Look at the map to find your area, then match its pattern to the key above. When you've found your color, the key will tell you what hardiness zone you live in. Remember that the map is a general guide; your particular conditions may vary.